To Harvey Rubenstein

A legal colloque

of long

standing

William Perlett

Oct 16, 2001

RISK
IN THE
AFTERNOON

RISK
IN THE
AFTERNOON

SOME OF THE PLEASURES AND PERILS
OF FOXCHASING

BY WILLIAM PRICKETT

RED FOX PUBLISHING

RED FOX PUBLISHING

Published by William Prickett a/k/a Red Fox Publishing Co.
4466 Summit Bridge Road, Middletown, Delaware 19709
(For additional copies, call 302. 876.0908)

Library of Congress Cataloging-in-Publication Data
Prickett, William
Risk in the Afternoon – Some of the Pleasures and
Perils of Fox Hunting
ISBN 0-9665352-0-0 Hardcover
1.Risk in the Afternoon – Sport   [1. Risk in the Afternoon]
I. Title
Library of Congress Catalog Card No. 98-091616

Designed by Cristina Lazar

Printed in Hong Kong through PrintNet

Proceeds will be used to support the Red Fox.

CONTENTS

PART ONE

INTRODUCTION

ME AND HORSES

by Betsy James Wyeth

Horses were never a part of my childhood, but they were very much a part of my sister Gwendolyn's life. One bright Sunday afternoon, she convinced me to give riding a try.

She assured me, when we arrived at the stables, that the one she chose for me to ride was very, very docile. "He just likes to walk, Betsy." To me he looked enormous as someone gave me a hand up. True to her words, we started out walking down the shoulder of a tarred road with a scattering of cars out for afternoon drives. This went on for quite a long time and I had just begun to enjoy being above it all when Gwen gave her horse a kick, leaving me far behind. Not to be outdone by my older sister, I gave Tony a gentle kick.

All hell broke loose. Tony went into a full gallop. Both of my feet came out of the stirrups, reins fell from my hands as down the middle of the road I flew. Cars pulled off the road. Horns honked, and Gwen reported later I went by her screaming, "Whoa, Tony! Whoa, Tony! Whoa, Tony!" Then he turned around and galloped back down the middle of the road we had just ridden up—me hanging on for dear life with my arms around his neck heading back to his stable. I have a vague memory of a stable hand running and yelling—then all goes blank after I hit my head on a low beam. That's the first and last time I ever rode a horse.

The next incident was related to me by my husband, Andrew. He had discovered a deep valley about a mile's walking distance from his Chadds Ford studio. Loaded down with a fishing tackle box in one hand and a block of paper under his other arm, he followed a winding stream up the valley until he came to a quiet pool where autumn leaves

Master of the Hounds, Water color by Andrew N. Wyeth (from the collection of the Hotel DuPont, Wilmington, Delaware).

floated on the surface. He sat down on the bank and made a pencil drawing before switching to watercolor. He supported the large block of paper on his lap, opened the tackle box full of brushes, paint tubes, rags and his pallet and a lunch I had packed for him. Lost in the mysterious act of creating, he began to paint. The only sound came from the gurgling brook. Later, he did remember hearing the sound of a hunting horn in the far distance but thought nothing of it. Perhaps an hour went by when, all of a sudden, the baying of hounds filled the valley, and before he knew it a whole pack of hounds came rushing down the steep slope, knocking him over, licking his face, upsetting the tackle box, paint tubes flying, brushes floating down the stream and ending by tramping all over his half-completed watercolor with muddy paws. The only thing that survived was the pencil drawing secured inside of the pad he had been sitting on. The hounds even gobbled up his lunch. Bedraggled, he retrieved what he could and set out for home.

Heavy rains fell for a week. When he went back, the stream had changed its course and all the leaves were gone.

A few years later, Frolic Weymouth came into the family bringing his horses and carriages with him. He was aware of my thing about horses but one day said, "Come on Bets, you've got to get over it. How about going to the Radnor Horse Show with me? It's great fun and we can sit in Ma's box as she's not going." The day arrived, Frolic picked me up and off we went. Just before the show began, his mother arrived and, in no uncertain terms, let it be known she needed every seat in her box for her guests. We ended up in the bleachers or standing close to the track, which was fine with me.

The events began. The first race was on. Excitement filled the air when the horses reached the point where we were standing. One handsome horse stumbled and hit the ground, dead, and had to be loaded onto a flat bed to be carried off. Frolic took me home, which brings me to my final horse affair.

I love to bet. Just crazy about it—so Dr. Margaret Handy took me to the races at Delaware Park. I figured we would be far enough away from the track if some terrible event happened. Nothing doing—she had tickets, or whatever, and ended up almost on the track. We placed our bets, the loud speaker blared, the race began. The horse I had placed my bet on was neck and neck up forward when something happened. It fell and broke its leg and had to be shot directly in front of us.

By now, you must understand my misgivings when our lawyer and good friend, Bill Prickett, asked if I would read his manuscript for *Risk in the Afternoon*. By the time I reached the second chapter, I was hooked. Believe me, it is a wonderful account by a man who loves foxhunting (or foxchasing) with all his heart and soul. I not only learned a lot but ended his accounts by envying anyone who dares to take up this fascinating, challenging and truly rewarding sport. You have a thoroughly enjoyable experience ahead of you.

Betsy James Wyeth
New Year's Day, 1998

Comment by Mrs. John B. Hannum, MFH
of Mr. Stewart's Cheshire Hounds

February 10, 1998

Bill,

You have paid me an enormous compliment by asking me to review this book and change anything not accurate. In Mrs. Wyeth's Foreword, which is a perfect start to your treatise on foxhunting, she refers to Frolic[1] taking her to the "Radnor Horse Show." This should be written "Radnor Hunt Race Meeting."

Otherwise, all is outstanding!

Nancy Hannum

---

[1]George A. ("Frolic") Weymouth of Chadds Ford, Pennsylvania, has been a foxhunter, show rider, polo player and is a carriage driver, painter, portraitist, founder and still chairman of the Brandywine River Museum, and principal architect of conservation of the Brandywine Valley (and a longtime friend of the author.)

DEDICATION

There are several reasons why I have the audacity to collect and publish an explanation of foxhunting and some accounts of my own foxhunting over the years. First, since I am now over seventy and have two artificial knees (but can and do still foxhunt), it is a pleasure for me to set out to relive some of the fun and excitement that I have had over the years in pursuing the ellusive red fox. Thus, if for no other reason, I write simply for my own enjoyment and for the enjoyment of you, my readers.

Second, I write to try to explain to any layman who is willing to read what I write what foxhunting is all about. Foxhunting is widely misunderstood in America. Most laymen, knowing very little about foxhunting, think that foxhunters are a group of drunken male elitists who gallop ruthlessly over poor farmers' crops without permission, following cruel savage hounds who tear harmless little foxes to pieces and then devour the pieces. As will be shown, not a single word of the previous sentence is true. Others think foxhunting is slightly comic, anachronistic and silly. It is none of the foregoing: it is tough and may be downright dangerous, but, above all, it's great fun.

Third, I write to try to express my thanks to all those who have made these weekly respites from reality possible for me: that is, tedious legal work, financial worries and all the other troubles that are everyone's lot in real life. At the top of this list come the Masters of Foxhounds, as well as the Huntsmen, the Whips, and Field Masters whom I have tried to follow. Next must come such friends as Bob Peoples who first got me to take up foxhunting, Peter Winants, M.F.H., who first lent and then gave me hunting horses, Rowe O'Neal who was my first mentor on foxhunting, and finally Nancy Miller who now enables me to continue to foxhunt long after I would otherwise have had to hang up my

Mrs. John B. Hannum, MFH, Cheshire Hounds. Photographer: Freudy Photos, New York, New York.

tack (quit hunting). I hasten to include my thanks to all of the many foxhunters, some but by no means all of whom will appear by name in these pages, whose sporting fellowship has helped make fox hunting such a pleasure over the years. In this connection, the question inevitably came up as to whether I would try to mention by name all of the many friends with whom I enjoyed hunting over the years. The risk, on the one hand, was leaving out someone. The risk, on the other hand, was just writing out long lists of names. Space considerations preclude me from including most of the names of those I have hunted with, but surely those who have hunted with me, if they read this, will recognize shared experiences.

Head and shoulders above all stands the indomitable and legendary Mrs. John B. Hannum, for fifty seasons the Master of Foxhounds of the Cheshire Hounds. She is the epitome of the best of foxhunting. She has devoted her life to foxhunting. For more than four decades, she herself carried the horn as the Master of the Cheshire Hounds, always well turned out, hunting her beautifully bred pack of English hounds and fearlessly leading her field of foxhunters with the help of Field Masters and whips. She is still very much the Master, but reluctantly she had to give up carrying the horn herself after so many bone crushing falls that there literally was not a bone in her relatively small body that had not been broken several times. But, when the time to lead the sport from the back of her horse necessarily came to an end, Mrs. Hannum did not give foxhunting up, retire to her beautiful house, Brooklawn, to pursue more sedentary and personal pleasures. On the contrary, she redoubled her efforts to provide sport for others, such as myself.

Thus, she is up at the crack of dawn year around seeing that the hunt staff horses are gotten out and exercised, that young hounds are schooled and the pack trained, and that the fields, paths, fences and relationships with landowners and farmers in the hunting country are kept up. She is there at all hunts in her somewhat battered Jeep, the back door of which is at times held closed with bailing twine. At the meets, in Bean boots and a worn parka, she confers with her Huntsman, Joe Cassidy, as well as the whips, Larry Snyder and Monk Crossan, Anthony Jenks, and, on occasion, Ramsey Buchanan and Chip Miller. The Field Master, Bruce Miller, is included as are alternative Field Masters, Mrs. Hannum's sons, Jock and Buzzy, Stephanie Speakman, and Nancy Miller. The counsel of foxhunters, farmers and countrymen knowledgeable in the ways of the foxes and foxhunting is sought.

Mrs. Hannum then decides and directs the strategy for that day's hunt, assessing not only the country to be hunted, every inch of which she knows by heart, but the temperature and conditions for scent, the wind's strength and direction, and the known or reputed location of foxes seen or rumored to be abroad in the country and many, many other factors, all of which go into creating a successful hunt. She then leads, follows and helps the hunt from her Jeep. She can often be heard in the course of an afternoon with the voice of a Valkyrie hallooing a fox she has viewed (seen) from the top of a hill,

Mrs. John B. Hannum, MFH, Cheshire Hounds. Photographer: Freudy Photos, New York, New York.

summoning the hounds, the hunting staff and the field, and putting them onto the line which the fox has taken. Her sole reward for all this work and devotion is the paltry thanks of those for whom she creates so much pleasure. Aside from a necessary contribution to support the hunt, the only thing that Mrs. Hannum really asks of a foxhunter is a stout horse and a stout heart (the courage to follow where the fox and the hounds lead).

As a matter of fact, I have repeatedly urged Mrs. Hannum, without success, to write a book on foxhunting. Now, there would be a real volume that would tell us all about every aspect of foxhunting, including the mysteries of scent, the bloodlines of hounds and hunting horses, the ways of foxes, the strategy of conducting a foxhunt and many other aspects of foxhunting which will not appear in this volume, both because of space limitations and because of my limited knowledge and experience. This book is no substitute: it consists only of a series of recollections by "a run and jump" Saturday foxhunter. Any really knowledgeable foxhunter will get precious little or nothing at all from this book except perhaps the shared excitement of the recollections of foxhunting.

Though it will not add one iota to Mrs. Hannum's stature or reputation, I dedicate this volume to her with respect, gratitude and affection.

Joe Cassidy, Huntsman, with the Cheshire Hounds.
Photographer: James Graham.

APOLOGIES TO ERNEST HEMINGWAY

The real justification for this book is to try to explain just what foxhunting is about to those who have never been lucky enough to do it themselves. I do so in part to try to help stem the criticism of foxhunting generated by people who, knowing little about foxhunting, seek to outlaw foxhunting completely in the United States, just as the British Labor Party seems to have tried to do in England.

However, the actual genesis of this book came late one cold Saturday afternoon in February a year or so ago. I was to meet my wife, Caroline, who does not foxhunt herself but who encourages me to do so, at her sister Diana Lopez's house. I came to the Lopez front door and knocked.

As she opened the door and saw my telltale muddy boots and hunting clothes, Diana's big dark eyes widened. Her usually radiant countenance quickly clouded over. She exclaimed with real pain in her voice, "Bill, I do hope that you have had fun today but that the foxes all got away safely. Tell me quickly but truthfully you didn't kill any foxes, did you?"

I responded, "We had a truly wonderful day. I assure you that we did not kill any foxes. Though I don't think you believe me, we are not out to kill foxes. We just like to find and chase the red fox. A good day for us is one when the hounds first find a good red fox and then chase the fox for miles over the hills and valleys of Unionville. Then, the fox, when he has had enough, pops down into the safety of a hole. That's what happened today."

Diana replied uneasily, "I see." But, I could tell from her averted eyes that she really didn't believe me.

John, her husband, a passionate trout fisherman, led me on in. John smiled as he

William Prickett on Yank. Photographer: Unknown.

poured me a glass of good red wine. He raised his own glass and said, "As Oscar Wilde so aptly toasted foxhunting, here's to the unspeakable who hunt and kill the uneatable!"

I said, "John, foxhunters don't try to kill foxes any more than real fly fishermen try to kill trout. They release the trout unharmed. Similarly, foxhunting is the sport of finding and chasing foxes."

Again, I could sense doubt as John smiled again and said, "Yes, well, maybe." I drank my wine and said nothing more. I realized I had not been able to persuade either of them and many others that the objective of a foxhunter is not the killing of foxes.

Perhaps I never will. But if any laymen will just take the time to read this book, then they will come to understand that foxhunters are not out to kill the foxes they chase with such pleasure. Rather, foxhunters enjoy the excitement, the risks, and the pleasures of finding and chasing, but not catching, much less killing, the beautiful, wily and elusive red fox.

The title of this book, *Risk in the Afternoon*, is clearly a change of the title of Ernest Hemingway's great work about bullfighting entitled *Death in the Afternoon*. But, you, the reader, might well point out that this book is about foxhunting, not bullfighting. First, let me suggest: if you haven't read *Death in the Afternoon*, then put this book down right now and go get the real McCoy, just as quickly as you can. Why? For three reasons. First, *Death in the Afternoon* is great fun to read. Second, if you have never read *Death in the Afternoon*, it seems to me you may have slighted your own literary education. The last reason is that this book will make better sense if you are familiar with *Death in the Afternoon*. (Thus, do not go any further with this book: I am quite content to wait until you have finished the original.)

If you, the reader, have done what I asked you to do, you have now made the acquaintance of the Old Lady with whom Mr. Hemingway discussed everything to do with bullfighting. (With your kind permission, the balance of this chapter will consist of a discussion with this opinionated Old Lady about foxhunting.)

The Old Lady: "Sir, what right do you have to try to bring attention to your book by playing a change on the title of *Death in the Afternoon*?"

"I grew up reading Mr. Hemingway. I like his grand writing style and his clear use of the English language. I like his humor and his digressions. I have always admired his macho approach, even though it is now the goal of lesser authors, academics, critics and would-be biographers to try to tear the old man apart. Thus, I frankly copy and adopt from an heroic model."

Old Lady: "So you like Mr. Hemingway? So do I. But surely that doesn't explain why you have brazenly made a word play on Mr. Hemingway's title. What in the world does bullfighting have to do with foxhunting?"

"Mr. Hemingway titled his book *Death in the Afternoon* because bullfights and, hence, injury or death typically takes place in the late afternoon in the bullring. This book is entitled *Risk in the Afternoon* because, though foxhunting typically starts at 11 a.m., the risk of injury from falls is greatest in the late afternoon when the shadows lengthen and horses and riders tire after a hard day of galloping for miles and jumping over fences."

Old Lady: "Very interesting, but just what is the similarity between fighting bulls and foxhunting?"

"There is in fact a basic similarity. As you know, Mr. Hemingway's book is really about the risk to the bullfighter, or more properly the torrero, of getting gored. There is always the ultimate possibility of a torrero's death in the bull ring. Further, when one has read Mr. Hemingway's book, one cannot help but come away knowing that bullfighting is really an art involving form, drama and ritual. It is not the cruel slaughter of bulls to satisfy blood lust. Thus, one central focus of Mr. Hemingway's book is about the great risk involved to the torreros and the near certainty that they will be severely gored or killed outright during their careers."

Old Lady: "I and all Mr. Hemingway's readers know all about the risks to the torreros. So, let's get back to foxhunting. What in the world does the risk of bullfighting have to do with foxhunting?"

"Foxhunting also involves risk of injury or even death."

Old Lady: "Tell me, what risks, are you talking about and to whom?"

"First, the fox risks death every time he voluntarily decides to leave the safety of his nearby hole and, instead, leads a baying pack of hounds across the hills and fields, often pausing until the hounds almost catch up to him. The red fox deliberately courts this risk of death. No one really knows why the red fox thus flirts with death. The red fox, not originally native to the U.S. but brought over from England by sporting Colonials in mid-Seventeenth Century, has always been hunted with hounds in America. For instance, George Washington and Billy Lee, his Huntsman, were avid foxhunters."

Old Lady: "Obviously, the fox clearly does take a great risk, but no one else does."

"Wrong, wrong, wrong. Besides the risk to the fox, there is always risk to those who try to follow the fox and the hounds. It is almost a very real certainty that every foxhunter will suffer at least one fall per season. With bad luck and unavoidable accidents, a foxhunter may have half a dozen falls in one year. This is not just wobbling and comically tumbling off as many non-riders seem to think with safe amusement."

Old Lady: "Does a fall always result in an injury?"

"No, but every fall carries with it the possibility of everything from a simple jolt to disabling injury, such as a broken collarbone or leg or a concussion. Indeed, it is certain that I will suffer a couple of falls between the time of our conversation and the time this is published. In addition, there are also every season reports of death in the hunting field somewhere in the United States. For example, a couple of years ago, my dear friend, Dr. Gordon French, with whom I had traded off-color stories for years while hunting, suffered a fatal fall when his horse stumbled while coming down a steep hill following the Cheshire Hounds. Dr. French broke his neck and died instantly."

Old Lady: "How tragic!"

"Not quite. Gordon was in his seventies and doing what he liked doing best. A clean quick death might well have been acceptable to Gordon (and indeed to me)."

Old Lady: "Tell me more about your falls."

"Okay, everyone likes to hear about other peoples' falls. Falls are inevitable in riding, especially in hunting. But, they are rarely the result of simply losing one's balance and falling off. Rather, falls generally are the result of accidents. For example, many years ago, I was just about to jump Yank, an able-bodied crossbred gelding, over a fence. Right ahead of me on the far side of the fence was a young girl on her pony. She, having safely cleared the fence, was undecided whether to turn right or left, so she stopped dead in her tracks for just a moment. Yank had started his jump but swerved to the left in mid-air at the very last instant and managed to avoid coming smack dab down on top of the hapless pony and rider. The youngster never looked back but turned right and trotted off. I got dumped and broke my right leg. She, to this day, probably does not know that her momentary hesitation was literally my downfall. She probably thought my fall was due to poor horsemanship, as it might well have been.

"Another time, I was galloping a stout mare, Fanny, across a beautiful field in pursuit of Stanchfield Wright, the Master of Vicmead at the time. The Master, in turn, was following the Huntsman who was following the hounds. Too late, I heard the warning cry 'Ware Hole!' (beware of a hole such as a groundhog hole). Fanny, who like most good hunting horses kept a wary eye out for holes, saw one, dodged to miss it and put her big foot squarely in another hole. Fortunately, she was able to bend her knee in time and not break a leg but she turned upside down, throwing me forward out of the saddle and onto the ground. I suffered a pair of cracked ribs, nothing more serious.

"Then, one cold January day at Unionville about ten years after my fall with Fanny, Fanny's colt, Tug, and I were galloping smartly around the edge of a woods on top of a high hill in the Saturday country (that is, the country usually hunted on Saturdays as contrasted with the Unionville Tuesday country or Thursday country). The going underfoot for the horses had been good but, in the shadow of the far side of the woods, there was still a sheet of white ice. As Tug and I came pelting around the corner going hell for leather behind the hounds who were now in full cry and already crossing the valley below, Tug's feet flipped right out from under him. Tug floundered a couple of seconds, all four feet thrashing, but on down he went, dumping me on my head. I was knocked cold briefly and had a concussion. Mercifully, I was wearing a caliente riding helmet and did not suffer a serious injury. Tug himself was none the worse for our spill."

Old Lady: "You make it sound like you get injured every time you go out."

"No, not all. Falls are the unfortunate exception, not the rule. There are lots of falls that do not result in anything serious. The point is, however, that there is always risk. Any one of the above accidents could have resulted in far more serious injury. There are falls that do result in serious injuries. One ardent foxhunter's horse stepped in a totally invisible groundhog hole; she broke her back and was in a plaster cast from her feet to her neck and then had traction and a brace for eighteen months. As soon as she could, she went right back to hunting again. One of the ablest riders in the whole Cheshire field, suffered a head injury when her horse's feet went out from under him on a bit of slippery asphalt while galloping around the corner of a barn. Joe Cassidy, Unionville's hard riding Huntsman, is in constant nerve pain as a result of having his knee smashed against an oak tree while galloping after his hounds. A show rider and foxhunter broke both her collarbone and shoulder when she reached up to pat her horse for jumping nicely over a tricky fence. Her horse chose that moment to put in a mighty buck; off she went and, as I say, broke her shoulder and her collarbone."

Old Lady: "But let's get back to risks. The risks in bullfighting are also serious, as we all know."

"Yes, but the active risk in foxhunting is quite different from watching bulls being fought by professional torreros. Neither Mr. Hemingway nor other critics or spectators incur any personal risk whatsoever sitting in safety behind the barrio up in the grandstand while criticizing the style and bravery of the torreros. The torreros take all the deadly risk of fighting and singlehandedly killing ferocious bulls with nothing more than a cape and a small sword."

Old Lady: "Do stop, for pity sake! I have heard quite enough criticism about Mr. Hemingway. He was a great literary figure and an old friend of mine. I have a good mind to stop reading this book right here and now!"

"Well, stop, if you want to, but let me quickly add, to avoid getting pelted with literary cushions before I can properly get started, one of Mr. Hemingway's principal points is applicable. He said, in effect, 'Reject bullfighting if you must, but before you reject it, you should at least try to understand what it is all about.' In other words, Mr. Hemingway pointed out one should go and see and try to understand bullfighting rather than simply rejecting bullfighting out of hand without knowing anything about it. Similarly, one should ride to hounds to learn what foxhunting is about. But not everyone is as fortunate as I have been; that is, to have the wonderful opportunity to foxhunt all my adult life. So that is what this book will attempt to do—explain in plain understandable English to laymen what foxhunting is all about and why it is that I and so many others have joyously accepted its very real risks for years."

Old Lady: "I for one am glad to hear that you will try to write plainly so that this book will be understandable. So, tell me a little something about foxhunting."

"To begin with, foxhunting is misunderstood in America. People who are not familiar with it say they are appalled at the wanton cruelty of foxhunting."

Old Lady: "What you really do is to go out to kill foxes, don't you? Isn't that what you really do?"

"No, American foxhunters are not really out to kill foxes."

Old Lady: "What! What do you mean you don't kill foxes? I think you are trying to pull my leg! Why, everyone knows that you do kill cute little foxes. I am sure you kill foxes in droves!"

"No, not at all. We certainly do not kill foxes in droves. On the contrary, we kill very, very few foxes. Actually, the word foxhunting is really a misnomer. Foxchasing is more accurate. The sport lies in watching a well disciplined pack of hounds efficiently hunt through a woodland in an orthodox manner (spread out effectively to cover a wide area, always conscious of the direction their Huntsman wishes them to follow). They concentrate their search for only the scent of a fox, disregarding all other game, and also listen for the encouraging single note on the Huntsman's horn and the sound of his voice directing them in a sing-song fashion to 'go in there, rouse him up.' This is how a fox is found. Then with a chorus of music as each hound's cry mingles with the pack, they pursue their clever, wily fox in his game of hide and seek until he tires and seeks the safety of his earth (a hole in the ground)."

Old Lady: "Do you really mean to tell me that the fox participates in foxhunting, or foxchasing as you call it?"

"Oh, yes. The fox has always been a willing participant in foxchasing. Quite often the hounds will find a fox quite near the fox's own hole or den. The fox could perfectly well simply pop right on down his hole. Then there is virtually nothing that a pack of hounds and the foxhunters can do at that point except go home or look for another fox. Foxhounds are far too big to follow a fox down its hole or den. However, quite often, a red fox will deliberately leave the safety of his nearby hole and lope across the fields and woods ahead of the hounds. Some times a fox will even stop, sit on his haunches and watch the hounds as the hounds attempt to follow him, not by sight, but by sniffing his scent."

Old Lady: "What happens if you don't find a fox?"

"That sometimes happens. It is called a blank day. The foxhunters must content themselves with the pleasures of a day out in the open, enjoying the countryside on horseback. Incidentally, a true foxhunter may well not be at all interested in the riding aspects of foxhunting. To a real foxhunter, the riding and jumping are entirely incidental—simply the only way to stay with the hounds."

Old Lady: "But, don't the hounds see the poor fox?"

"No. Foxhounds have decent eyesight, but they hunt with their noses. The hounds hunt mostly by following the strong scent that a fox throws off."

Old Lady: "When the hounds get on the fox's trail, then what happens?"

"Then the fox will scamper, slither or lope away. He will often foil the hounds by running on top of fallen logs, by running through a plowed field or a field on which horse or cow manure has been freshly spread, or by running down a road where his scent will not stick. A clever fox will suddenly jump at right angles off a road and go off into the honeysuckle or the fields. Sometimes a fox runs right down the middle of a stream where his scent will not lie and then jump out a couple of hundred yards on down. These tricks, of course, throw the hounds off. Sometimes a fox will run through a herd of cattle. Here again, the hounds are thrown off the fox's scent. At times he will double right back for some little distance. Thus, the hounds will be sniffing in the wrong direction."

Old Lady: "Tell me, does the red fox run in a straight line?"

"No. Deer, on the other hand, do run in a straight line and thus often go right on out of the hunting country. That is one reason why foxhunters dislike deer and never allow foxhounds to hunt them. But, a characteristic of the red fox is that he usually runs in a circle or a figure eight. A fox will make some sort of a circle and generally come back to the area from which he started. Masters, the Huntsman, and knowledgeable foxhunters, of course, are totally familiar with this basic characteristic. Part of the art of foxchasing is trying to figure out which way and when the fox will turn. Of course, the diameter of the fox's circle can and does vary widely—anywhere from 500 yards to three or four miles. That means that while the knowledgeable foxhunter knows the fox is going to turn at some point either right or left, the foxhunter does not know when or where the is fox going to make his turn, whether he will turn left or right, or how large the circle or loop will be."

Old Lady: "Does the red fox always come back to where he started and go down his hole?"

"Quite often he will in fact do just that—start from his hole, go out and make a big circle, come back and go right down the very hole he had originally left. At other times, the fox will come back and go on right past the hole he originally started from and will then make another circle out in another direction and then come back to his hole. On the other hand, the fox may at any time go down another hole, either in the vicinity of his original hole or find a friendly refuge along the way if he is tired or if the hounds are getting too close for comfort."

Old Lady: "But aren't the hounds much bigger and faster than the little fox? Don't they usually catch the fox and tear him to shreds?"

"No, no, that's just not the way it is. In the first place, the hounds are bred in size so as to be able to just about keep up with a healthy red fox. A good fox can run with amazing speed in open country and with incredible agility through the woods and tangled thickets. A healthy fox can usually outdistance a pack of hounds simply by running. Foxhounds hunt almost always by scent, not by seeing the fox as foxhunters do. As I have said, the fox can throw the hounds off his track by dozens of tricks that every fox seems to know."

Old Lady: "But you still have not answered me. Don't the hounds always, or at least usually, manage to end up catching the fox, killing it and then devouring it?"

"Though you will probably be surprised, the answer is no. I have been foxhunting on fall and winter Saturdays for more than forty years. In all that time I have been in on outright kills of healthy foxes hunted by hounds no more than twenty times."

Old Lady: "What! You mean in all that time you have been in on kills only once every two years or so. I frankly do not believe you. Until this very moment, I had always believed that you killed loads of foxes each time you went out hunting."

"Well, you and many others are mistaken. But, just ask any American foxhunter if you do not to believe me. The real thrill of the sport is in first finding and then chasing the fox, not in killing it. The kill of a fox, as occasionally happens, is a sad anticlimax for the huntsmen, foxhunters, and indeed the hounds themselves."

Old Lady: "Only twenty foxes in forty years seems like a very paltry number indeed!"

"It is a very small number. Remember, I am talking only about the United States. But, still, one of the greatest fallacies about foxhunting in the United States is the widespread belief that it consists of the wholesale killing of foxes. Nothing could be further from the truth. Really, the sport is foxchasing, not killing foxes."

Old Lady: "Well, I never. I always thought you people killed tons of foxes as pests or nuisances!"

"Oh, no, no, no. Foxes are not pests. On the contrary, foxes are beautiful, exotic animals. The sight of a red fox is always electrifying. Besides, if foxhunters really wanted to kill foxes, they could do it far more efficiently with poison or traps or guns. Even if one wanted to kill foxes with hounds, a much surer way of killing them would be to sneak up to a woods or covert noiselessly and then surround the covert with a tight ring of hounds and foxhunters. When the fox sought to escape, the fox would find himself surrounded and would be turned back to the hounds. Then, of course, the fox would certainly be killed. But, that is never, never done. On the contrary, it is a cardinal sin for any laggard member of the hunt to get in such a position that he 'turns' a fox. That is why foxhunters are continually admonished to stay behind the Field Master but to stay up close enough so as not to inadvertently turn a fox."

Old Lady: "Just what does turning a fox mean?"

"That means a fox is forced to turn back and has to face the hounds and then try to run the gauntlet of the hounds."

Old Lady: "Who or what does turn foxes?"

"Foxes are often turned by others than laggard foxhunters. For instance, car followers do turn foxes at times."

Old Lady: "Does anything or anyone else turn foxes?"

"Yes indeed, farm machinery, people afoot, such as bird watchers, lovers or hikers."

Old Lady: "What can be done to protect foxes?"

"Well, of course, if one were really interested in protecting foxes, one would first outlaw all cars, school busses and trucks in the country where foxes live. Why so, you ask? Because we have all seen far many more foxes smashed and flattened by motor vehicles in one year than have been killed by hounds in decades. Indeed, foxhunters feed foxes and protect the fox population against disease, such as rabies and mange."

Old Lady: "I see. This conversation has been interesting."

"Incidentally, you say you understand all about bullfighting as a result of Mr. Hemingway's book. But consider the fact that in bullfighting six bulls are killed in an afternoon. The killing of bulls is the whole point of bullfights. But in foxhunting, on the contrary, the object is not to kill the fox but only to chase the fox. The killing of a fox is the exception and is almost always the result of an accident or mistake rather than an intended result."

Old Lady: "You may have a point. I never thought of that."

"I have enjoyed talking to you and trying to explain something to you about the glorious sport of chasing foxes. By the way, are you by chance an admirer of Winston Churchill?"

Old Lady: "Yes, I certainly am. Winston always will stand head and shoulders above the pygmies who now strut about while fumbling with the world's destiny."

"I suspected you would be a Churchill fan. Did you know Churchill once said, 'If there is a more admirable and elevating sport than foxhunting, it has yet to be discovered.' "

Old Lady: "Did Churchill really say that? That's very interesting."

"Madam, indeed he did. Thank you for your help. I am quite sure our discussion has been invaluable to my readers just as your discussion with your friend, Mr. Hemingway, in *Death in the Afternoon* is invaluable to an understanding of bullfighting."

MY RECURRENT DREAM

On top of a wind swept hill not far from Unionville, Pennsylvania, the figure of a small white haired woman in a faded parka and Bean boots can be seen outlined against the bright blue sky striding around a somewhat battered blue Jeep station wagon. A small brown Jack Russell terrier bounds and frisks about her. Winter is over, but there are still traces of snow in shady spots. Clouds sail majestically along overhead, driven by the blustery March wind. The pale yellow winter sun is about to set. The trees are totally bare, but there is a hint of incipient spring in the form of bright little green sprigs of skunk cabbage that peep up here and there along the edge of the icy brook running through the valley lying around the foot of the hill.

The Huntsman has just cast his pack of black, brown and white English hounds into the heavy underbrush along the stream. In and out of thickets and second growth the hounds can be seen silently but feverishly working, weaving in and out, their sterns or tails wagging briskly, their noses pressed to the ground sniffing this way and that for the delightful elixir of the scent of a fox who earlier had been reported going about his business in these parts: it was the large red fox hunted several times before this fall and winter who is reputed to den down somewhere in this vicinity. The red-coated Huntsman supervises and encourages his hounds by cheery calls to them now and then. The windy silence of the late afternoon is also punctuated from time to time by an encouraging series of sharp notes on the Huntsman's short copper horn. A quarter of a mile away to the north on a small rise sitting on his horse is one of the Huntsman's "eyes and ears," that is a red-coated whip, outposted there to see if perhaps the fox, already alerted by the horn, will try to slide out in that direction out of the cover (woods or thicket). A quarter of a mile

Jack Trainer and Cheshire Field going over a stiff fence. Photographer: James Graham, Montchanin, Delaware.

around to the south and down by the stream, the other whip has posted himself, likewise looking for the fox, a flash of red with a bushy tail tipped with white, emerging at a lope from the undergrowth. A hundred and fifty feet back of the Huntsman sits the Field Master, gently holding back some forty eager foxhunters, mounted on all manner of horses and hunting ponies, chatting very quietly, waiting with obvious relish and subdued excitement for the fox chase they hope will soon begin. Some of the horses stand quietly enough while others, like mine, paw the ground and circle around restlessly. There is an atmosphere of restrained nervous tension and excitement.

All of a sudden, the expectant stillness is broken by a series of deep-throated halloos from the small figure at the top of the distant hill: her arm points directly to the far side of the covert. Clearly, she has viewed the fox coming out of the covert and trying to steal away from the hounds. The whip to the north instantly spurs his horse into a gallop in the direction where the fox has been seen. Then, not one hundred yards away on the far side of the stream, a beautiful red fox with a flowing tail tipped with white darts out of the undergrowth and lopes easily away from the stream and up the long hill. A half dozen foxhunters rise in their stirrups and point either with their hats or arms to the swift moving fox. The fox deliberately pauses once or twice to look behind. Then, veering to the right, the fox disappears from sight over the shoulder of the hill. The terrier just manages to jump into the old blue Jeep station wagon before it is wheeled sharply around and bumps and lurches away, as it too disappears over the crest of the hill but well clear of the path the fox has taken. The members of the field (the foxhunters) break into broad smiles, set their hats firmly and take up their reins: the horses' ears prick forward.

As soon as the halloo is sounded from the top of the hill, the call from the Huntsman's horn changes from inquiring and challenging notes to a series of sharp staccato blasts, signaling by its strident sounds to the hounds, the waiting foxhunters, and indeed the fox himself, that a fox has been viewed and is away. All of a sudden, the lead hound catches a small whiff of the intoxicating scent of the fox: he breaks into a glorious series of deep throated bays. Quickly the other hounds, hearing the lead hound, look up and honor him by assembling from all directions. These hounds in turn break into full cry when they too catch a whiff of the scent of the fox. The Huntsman, on seeing the fox, has to predict that the fox will go right-handed over the shoulder of the hill and also decide instantly on the best course for him to follow to try to stay with his hounds. The pack is already streaming pell-mell up the hill on the line of the fox with cascades of glorious baying echoing and reverberating from the surrounding hills. The Huntsman first puts his horse into a fast trot, then quickly spurs him into a gallop down the bank and, after splashing through the stream, gallops up the bank on the far side. The Huntsman heads for the stout three-rail fence that encloses the large hill. The Field Master follows the Huntsman, in turn leading the field of hard riding foxhunters, now all going toward the three-railer at a full gallop. The Huntsman steadies his racing horse as he approaches this stiff fence. The horse collects himself, then soars up and gracefully over the fence and gallops away up the hill. The Huntsman blows his horn as he goes. The hounds are now well on ahead, having disappeared over the shoulder of the hill following the fox. The Field Master successfully jumps over this formidable fence, right behind the Huntsman, closely followed by the first "flight" of the field. The other members of the field spread out, each rider picking a particular panel of the three-rail fence to jump. There is the thunderous noise of hoofbeats as the whole field gallops toward this fence.

Earlier in the season I had attempted to jump this very fence but my horse, following too closely on the heels of another horse, had begun his jump one stride too early: his hind feet had hit the top rail. My horse flipped forward, pitching me out of the saddle, over his head and onto the waiting grass. Thus, I now tighten my grip with my knees and steady my galloping horse. He perks his ears up and shorten his stride, measuring the fence as we roll toward this obstacle that we both remember so well. As we sweep on in, I fleetingly wonder whether we will clear this awesome fence or whether my horse will repeat our prior fall. Will he refuse at the last instant? Will he get in too close and hit the fence with his front feet or misjudge the fence and not clear it with his back feet, again dumping me on the ground? No time for such thoughts: we are only a stride out. Out of the corner of my left eye, I see a horse and rider at the next panel go cleanly and safely over. At the same time, I hear a loud crack to my right: someone has hit the fence. No time to look, I cross my reins, put one finger over my horse's martingale, lean well forward and give my horse his head by pushing the reins forward as he gets ready to jump. Finally, I "throw my heart over the fence" since any horse can sense instinctively whether the rider himself is going to jump or whether the rider is half afraid and hanging back from the impending jump . . .

The foregoing is designed to stir the interest of the reader, a little bit like an ice cold martini whets one's appetite before a good dinner or a private hand squeeze and a special little smile from a pretty woman at the playing of "Good Night Ladies" sets one's heart racing. But, if the reader's blood is not stirred by the foregoing and the reader is not interested in knowing what happened at that fence and indeed at the end of the hunt, then quietly close this book right here and now and pick up a sexy novel, spy thriller or a book by John Grisham. What follows is a very imperfect attempt to set out a few basic facts about foxhunting and a very personal explanation of why I have risked life and limb on fall and winter Saturdays for some forty years to enjoy the excitement and pleasure of chasing the elusive red fox. But, hold hard (stop right now): this will not be a long dry lecture or solemn tract on this challenging sport, though certain fundamentals will necessarily have to be mentioned in passing. The rudiments, however, will be included in rollicking accounts of fox hunts, horses, hounds, foxes, some of my spills (and the spills of others), and some of the colorful friends I have made in a lifetime of chasing foxes on Saturdays. I will try to explain why and how this sport has served me well by allowing me to escape briefly from the grinding, stressful and, at times, very boring life of a Delaware corporate trial lawyer, by testing and retesting my nerve, physical ability and stamina. These accounts are basically accurate, but please do not rein me in too tightly on all of the details: this book is not written with the exactitude of a legal brief. Rather, it is written principally for, the reader's pleasure as well as my own.

Now, if you are still with me, check and tighten your literary girth (make certain your saddle is secure), take a firm grip and let's gallop together, away from the pains and troubles of everyday life and escape briefly into the enchanted and exciting world of fox-hunting.

PART TWO

THE VICMEAD YEARS
1955-1976

THE VICMEAD HUNT CLUB

OPEN HOUSE

AND

SUPPER

THURSDAY, SEPTEMBER 7, AT 4:30

MIDDLE NECK ROAD

MIDDLETOWN, DELAWARE

THE VICMEAD YEARS
1955-1974

Originally organized about 1920, the Vicmead Hunt Club hunted the country in New Castle County north of Wilmington. After World War II, the Vicmead, because of suburban development, was forced to move down to the country lying west of Middletown, Delaware, roughly bounded on the north by the Chesapeake and Delaware Canal, on the south by the Little Bohemia Creek, on the west by the Maryland border, and on the east by Delaware Route 896. Basically flat, the country was made up of dairy, corn and soybean farms, laced by tidal and fresh water streams. The pastures and fields were interspersed with woods and second growth. Gradually the farms were replaced by horse racing and brood mare establishments whose activities necessarily restricted or precluded foxhunting.

In the late 1960s and early 1970s, many of the older members of the Vicmead retired from foxhunting: they were not replaced by younger members. Unfortunately, the Vicmead Hunt Club stopped foxhunting once and for all in 1980. By the time Vicmead stopped hunting, I had started hunting with Mrs. Hannum and the Cheshire Hounds in Unionville, Pennsylvania.

In Part Two, I recount some of the good times I had with Vicmead as I first began to go foxhunting.

Old men forget, yet all shall be forgot
But he'll remember with advantages
What feats he did that day
Then shall our names . . .
Be in their flowing cups freshly remembered.

SHAKESPEARE, HENRY V

MY FIRST HUNT

A horse, a horse, my Kingdom for a horse!
SHAKESPEARE, RICHARD III

It is now late August, but summer is still full upon us with all its heat and lushness. As always, at this time of year, my thoughts turn to the fall, to foxhunting and Opening Day, the first day of formal hunting. This was not always true. As a matter of fact, I took up riding only while at law school after a friendly orthopedist suggested riding or checkers as the alternatives to ending up in a wheelchair or on a walker if I had any more knee injuries. I therefore started riding a couple of times a week in the early mornings in a park near Harvard Law School.

I always thought that I would give up riding when I returned to Wilmington and really got into the practice of the law. Certainly, I never thought that I would go in for hunting. However, when I got back to Delaware, I took to renting a horse, Bob, from Rowe O'Neal and enjoying the Delaware and Pennsylvania countryside. Rowe had been a horseman all his life; he broke and trained horses; he had been a show rider; he had whipped hounds before World War II. On his discharge from the Army, Rowe became a jack of all trades in the horse world. He vanned show riders to horse shows and foxhunters to meets. He bought and sold horses and ponies. He regularly attended the horse auctions held every Monday at New Holland in the Amish country of Pennsylvania. He and his wife, Rose, had a small house and a trim little horse barn at Red Lion, Pennsylvania, on Street Road adjoining Longwood Gardens. Rowe commented on one of our easy jogs through the lovely countryside on a cool September morning that he expected that I would be foxhunting within the year. I disagreed forcefully, "Rowe, I will never foxhunt." Rowe smiled but said nothing more.

Rowe soon had me jumping small fences. One fine Saturday afternoon, we were quietly hacking (riding informally) through the Unionville country. The trees were all

William Prickett on Mistletoe. Photographer: Unknown.

aflame with color. Suddenly the stillness of the beautiful fall Saturday was broken: from far off came the faint sound of a Huntsman's horn. Soon a beautiful red fox bounded out of the woods. He loped easily away over the next hill; my first view was electrifying. Soon hounds came flying by in full cry followed by Mrs. Hannum, at the time still hunting her hounds. Her field, after a long run was strung out behind her. She called out as she galloped on past, "Come on now, Rowe, show your young friend something of foxhunting!" Bob was straining to be off with the hunt.

Rowe called back to her as she flew on by, "Thanks all the same, Ma'am, good hunting!"

As we ambled homeward, I asked, "Why didn't we join the hunt? After all, Mrs. Hannum herself invited us."

Rowe looked around at me, smiled and said, "Now ain't you the very same young fellah who swore not two weeks ago that you would never, never foxhunt? How about that?"

I said, "Aw, come on, Rowe."

The following spring, a friend of mine in Baltimore telephoned me and said that he wanted to dispose of an experienced hunting Morgan mare. He said, "I'll give you the Morgan because I want something classier, flashier, and with a tad more foot (speed). Will you take her off my hands?"

I replied with alacrity, "Indeed, I would love to!" Rowe was promptly dispatched to get the mare. I named the mare Mistletoe. I thought Mistletoe would be appropriate because I might often end up beneath her.

One of my close friends, Bob Peoples, had hunted for years with the Vicmead Hunt Club. Knowing I was riding out with Rowe, he had repeatedly urged me to take up hunting, promising that I would be welcome. I was not convinced. I was sure I would end up making a fool of myself, but I let myself be talked into trying foxhunting.

Before I could even consider going hunting, I had to take and pass the Delaware Bar exams. Once the exams were successfully behind me, I brought Mistletoe in from the pasture where she had been quietly grazing all summer. I had ridden her once or twice when she had come up from Maryland before she was turned out. She had seemed docile and knowledgeable—perfect. I had fashioned myself a stable out of an old, two-car garage, bought a secondhand saddle and some other tack. I was then ready to start training Mistletoe and myself in earnest for my first foxhunt.

After exercising her for a week or so, I decided it was time to see whether she and I could jump together. I put her at a low, two-rail fence. I did all the things Rowe had taught me to do when jumping a horse. Mistletoe moved willingly towards the fence. But, to my great surprise, at the very last moment, she stopped dead and did not go over the low fence. I almost went over her head. Turning her around, I headed her for the fence again. She did exactly the same thing. Finally, she stepped over it delicately, one foot at a time. We went on with our exercise.

I decided that the mare didn't like that one particular jump so I galloped her

William Prickett on Mistletoe. Photographer: Unknown.

towards a large log that lay across our path. She did exactly the same thing. By dint of kicking her hard, she finally gave a little jump and went over with about as much grace as a bullfrog.

Of course, I telephoned Rowe and told him that Mistletoe might be excellent as a hack or pleasure horse but she would never do as a serious hunting horse: she refused to jump.

Rowe replied quietly, "Mistletoe is a hunting mare. She will do well in the hunting field, mark my word." He added, "Don't expect her to fool around with practice, even though you need it." I had great confidence in Rowe, so I went on with the program of getting ready to hunt but without trying to school the mare over jumps.

I had never even seen a foxhunt (except for that brief time the fall before with Rowe). I knew the senior members of the hunt only slightly. It was therefore with a distinct sense of dread that I realized that the Saturday I had picked to try foxhunting for the first time was fast approaching. Bob Peoples continued to try to bolster my social and athletic courage, saying, "Foxhunting is great! You'll love it once you try it. You will receive a warm welcome even from older members." Like many things, once started, foxhunting was now inevitable even if it meant embarrassment and possibly coming home on a shutter.

To my somewhat persistent inquiries of Rowe, all he would say was, "Look, Mistletoe is a hunting mare. She knows her business." My silent reply was that she might have been a hunting mare at one time and known her business then, but, so far as I was concerned, she had never jumped anything with me, no matter how small, with any ease, willingness or sign of knowledgeability.

--Vicmead Hunt Club--
MARCH, 1969

Saturday	1	The Kennels	Noon
		Tea—Mr. and Mrs. William Pricket	
Tuesday	4	Old Bohemia Church	Noon
Thursday	6	Malmo	Noon
Saturday	8	Mr. Bayard Sharp's	Noon
		Middletown Pond Club invited to join Field	
Tuesday	11	Tybridge Farm	Noon
Thursday	13	Deer Crossing	Noon
Saturday	15	The Kennels	Noon
		Tea—Mrs. Carpenter, Brookdale Farm	
Saturday	22	The field is invited to hunt with the Pickering Hunt	
		Bryn Coed Farm	10:00
Friday	28	The Field is invited to hunt with Mr. Wilbur Ross Hubbard's Kent County Hounds	11:00

Landowners in the country of the Vicmead Hunt are always welcome.

The Field is requested to stay together, and to report promptly all broken rails to the Master.

Call the Kennels at Middletown, Del. 755-6918 if in doubt about weather.

From a Collection of Fixture Cards of the Vicmead Hunt Club.

All too soon, the fateful Saturday rolled around. The meet was at 8:00 A.M. Rowe appeared with his van at around 6:30 A.M. In a trice, the mare was loaded on the van and we were rolling down the highway towards the meet near Middletown, Delaware. I peppered Rowe with questions about the etiquette of hunting. To my discomfortiture, he gave only perfunctory replies to my questions. Of course, as I know now, there is nothing to all of this.

Another embarrassing detail lay in the fact that I did not know how to tie a stock (a long white cloth tied somewhat like a tie but with a flaring knot). I assumed that Rowe could tie a stock since he had been a whip and had ridden on Dilwyn's famous riding team. Rowe told me that he had no idea how to tie a stock since he always wore ready-tied stocks. It also turned out that my stock was some sort of an outlandish British stock. Nobody knew how to tie the thing. Needless to say, my appearance in secondhand boots, an old black coat, a badly tied stock and a seasoned derby hat left something to be desired.

When we arrived at the meet, Rowe pulled his van up among all the other vans. Through the early morning September mist, there was a welter of horses, riders and cars. Mistletoe came quietly enough out of the van. Her cooler was pulled off and her tack was adjusted. Rowe gave me a leg up and a reassuring clap on the leg and

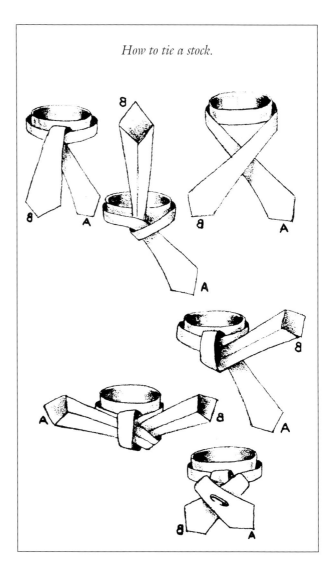

How to tie a stock.

said, "Good hunting, Lad." Mistletoe did not seem particularly excited by all the confusion, but I am sure that I more than made up for it. Through the fog came a series of notes from the Huntsman's horn. Soon I found myself trotting down a country road beside Bob Peoples. I was far too shy to say "Good Morning" to the Joint Masters as I should have. I did say a nervous hello to other members of the hunt. They all returned my greeting with a cheery phrase of welcome. I really appreciated these reassuring words.

But, inside of me was the annoying worry: did Mistletoe remember she was a hunting mare and she was supposed to jump? She had given some indications this morning that all that was going on was familiar to her, but that was not a definite sign she knew that she was expected to pick up her feet when she came to a fence. My confidence was not increased when a woman, whom I had known since second grade, came trotting up through the mist, took one look at me, did a doubletake, and blurted out "Good Lord, what in the world are you doing here?"

"At this point, that's exactly what I am wondering," I replied weakly.

There wasn't much time to think about all this because we were now close to a woods or covert. Chappie Frazer, the Huntsman, who had been sounding encouraging and inquiring notes on his short copper horn, suddenly changed his call. From ahead of us came a series of short staccato calls on the copper horn and the eager cries of the excited hounds. It was apparent, even to one who knew nothing about it, that we had found a fox.

Around me the desultory whispered chatter stopped, hats were firmly set and reins shortened. We trotted off in single file in the direction of the horn and the music of the hounds. Soon we broke into a brisk canter. Swinging around a clump of trees, I could see that our path lay down a gentle hill in the woods, then on through a small stream and out of the woods on the far side.

--Vicmead Hunt Club--
DECEMBER 1969

HOUNDS WILL MEET

Tuesday	2	Deer Crossing	Noon
Thursday	4	Back Creek	Noon
Saturday	6	Vicmead Field invited to Hunt with Monmouth County Hunt	11:00
Tuesday	9	The Kennels	Noon
Thursday	11	Old Bohemia Church	Noon
Saturday	13	Mr. Bayard Sharp's Jt. Meet—Mr. Jefford's Andrew's Bridge Hounds. Tea—Mr. and Mrs. Daniel Welford—Deepwell Farm	Noon
Tuesday	16	The Kennels	Noon
Thursday	18	Jt. Meet Pickering Hunt Pickering Country	11:00
Saturday	20	Deer Crossing	Noon
Tuesday	23	Malmo	Noon
		MERRY CHRISTMAS!—	No Hunting
Saturday	27	Bunker Hill Farm Middletown Pony Club invited to join field.	Noon
Tuesday	30	Mr. Bayard Sharp's	Noon

Landowners in the country of the Vicmead Hunt are always welcome to hunt.

The Field is requested to stay together, and to report promptly all broken rails to the Master.

Call the Kennels at Middletown, Delaware, 755-6918 if in doubt about weather.

At the far edge of the woods was a brand new three-rail fence, gleaming damply in the early morning light. There was, of course, a rider ahead of me and another behind me. There was no time to confide to these gentlemen that the horse I was riding probably had not recollected that she was supposed to be a hunting mare, and that I certainly wasn't a hunting man. There was no time for me to analyze my wet palms and the butterfly feeling in my stomach.

The horses picked up speed as they went down the long dip, splashed through the stream and came up on the other side. Looking towards this three-rail fence, I saw the riders ahead sailing over. Mistletoe was moving as she had never moved during our languid exercise sessions. Her ears were forward and she moved with grace and determination. As the rider in front of me took off and cleared the fence, I could feel my mare gathering herself under me and gauging her strides. I pushed the reins forward as Rowe had taught me, took a surreptitious hold of Mistletoe's mane, uncertain whether the mare was going to jump, stop, or simply plow through the fence.

She, of course, did know what she was supposed to do: she stood well back and sailed clean over the fence and went right on galloping on the other side. A grin broke over my face. I was hooked on foxhunting. The rest of the hunt was great. Mistletoe jumped thirty or so fences of various sizes and levels of difficulty. My only task was not getting in her way. She was, indeed, a good hunting mare who knew her business and loved it. I even viewed briefly and from afar the two fine foxes we hunted and "put to earth" (chased them until they went down into the safety of a hole). Rowe O'Neal beamed with pleasure when I dismounted. As he pulled up my stirrups and threw a cooler (a light blanket) over Mistletoe, he said "Well done, Lad."

After the hunt, I met and received the felicitations from the other members out that day. These and the other Vicmead riders came to be fast hunting friends in the years to come. I also did try to make amends by thanking the Joint Masters profusely. My belated tender of the capping fee was graciously refused by one of the lady Masters of Foxhounds who said, "Dear Boy, you and your dear little mare did very well indeed for your first day out foxhunting. You must promise to come every single Saturday from now on, and also on Tuesdays and Thursdays when you can escape from your law office and your strict

--Vicmead Hunt Club--
JANUARY 1970

HOUNDS WILL MEET

Thursday	1	The Kennels	11:00
Saturday	3	Tylridge Farm	Noon
		Joint Meet With New Market Hounds Tea—Mr. and Mrs. duPont—"The Rounds"	
Tuesday	6	Back Creek	Noon
Thursday	8	Old Bohemia Church	Noon
Saturday	10	St. Augustine	Noon
Tuesday	13	Mr. Bayard Sharp's	Noon
Thursday	15	The Kennels	Noon
Saturday	17	Joint Meet New Market Hounds	11:00
Tuesday	20	Malmo	Noon
Thursday	22	Deepwell Farm	Noon
Saturday	24	Old Bohemia Church	Noon
Tuesday	27	Back Creek	Noon
Thursday	29	Mr. Bayard Sharp's	Noon
Saturday	31	The Kennels	Noon
		Tea—Mr. and Mrs. Carpenter "Brookdale Farm"	

Landowners in the country of the Vicmead Hunt are always welcome to hunt.

The Field is requested to stay together, and to report promptly all broken rails to the Master.

Call the Kennels at Middletown, Delaware, 755-6918 if in doubt about weather.

father's watchful eye."

I thanked them for their invitation and promised to come every Saturday I could. (And, I did from that day forward.)

On the following day, I took the mare out to give her a little exercise. Gone was the fire and enthusiasm that had marked Mistletoe on the day before. Instead, she moved at a tepid pace. When we got to the first fence, she flatly refused to go over it. Indeed, when I forced her to jump, her jump was so halfhearted that she ended up straddling the fence. She was perfectly content to stay there, nibbling on the leaves of an overhanging tree until I dismounted and took the fence down around her and freed her up.

This was the pattern of things during the time that I had the mare. In the hunting field, Mistletoe was eager and determined, but she had no patience with schooling, especially jumping. She was a hunting mare and knew her business.

Some two years later, she went lame. Knowledgeable friends casually opined that the little mare would never come sound again (get over her lameness). I called my friend in Baltimore: he simply said, "Oh, go ahead and get rid of the mare. Sell her at New Holland. Get a classier hunter. Take my advice." I therefore sold Mistletoe to a horse dealer, truly believing she would never come sound again. Rowe disapproved my decision and quietly told me so, but I knew better. (Mistake, mistake, mistake.) I bought another horse named Dasher from the horse dealer. He represented to me that Dasher was an experienced hunting horse. As I had with Mistletoe, I waited until late August and then put Dasher into work. Like Mistletoe, Dasher had no taste for schooling. Dasher would jump but without any enthusiasm. Of course, by this time, I thought I knew a thing or two about the vagaries of hunting horses. Thus, I was not disturbed by Dasher's behavior. I just smiled knowingly.

Vicmead Hunt Club
JANUARY 1971

HOUNDS WILL MEET

Saturday	3	Deepwell Farm	Noon
Tuesday	5	Mr. Bayard Sharp's	Noon
Thursday	7	The Kennels	Noon
Saturday	9	Deer Crossing	Noon

Tea—Mr. and Mrs. William Prickett's

Tuesday	12	Malmo	
Thursday	14	Mr. William Ward's	Noon

Cherry Tree Rd.—Earleville Country

Saturday	16	St. Augustine	Noon

Joint meet with West Chester Hounds
Tea—Mr. and Mrs. Irenee May, Centerville, Pa.

Tuesday	19	The Kennels	Noon
Thursday	21	Mr. Bayard Sharp's	Noon
Saturday	23	Malmo	Noon

Tea—Mrs. Carpenter's Little House

Tuesday	26	Old Bohemia Church	Noon
Thursday	28	Bunker Hill Farm	Noon
Saturday	30	Back Creek	Noon

Landowners in the country of the Viemead Hunt are always welcome to hunt.

The Field is requested to stay together, and to report promptly all broken rails to the Master.

Call the Kennels at Middletown, Delaware, 755-6918 if in doubt about weather.

When Opening Day rolled around, I confidently pulled on my boots. I even wore a second-hand pink coat and top hat. (However, my stock still left a lot to be desired.) When the Huntsman blew his horn, indicating that we had found a fox, I was one of those pressing the Joint Masters, eager to be up with the hounds. As we galloped in towards the first fence, I smiled inwardly, thinking with smug assurance that now my new horse, Dasher, would surely remember that he was a hunting horse and would sail on over the fence, just as Mistletoe had sailed over our first fence together.

Alas, Dasher either never was a hunting horse or at least did not recollect that he was a hunting horse that day! He moved steadily and swiftly towards the fence, but Dasher never picked up his front feet at all or, for that matter, his back feet. We simply crashed right on through the fence. Dasher and I parted company, both doing cartwheels and ending up on the ground. The horse was not hurt, but I had fractured the wing bone in my shoulder, my top hat was crushed, and my pink coat was covered with dirt.

As I recovered from the surgery on my fractured wing bone, I wryly concluded that there was still a lot that I had to learn about foxhunting and hunting horses (I still do). I also remembered that Rowe had never told me that Dasher was a hunting horse.

It is August again and I am, of course, thinking of hunting. As I look out the window, I see another new horse contently switching flies and munching the green grass. I wonder if, when hunting rolls around, he will turn out to be a hunting horse.

You, the reader, might well ask, "Well, what happened to Mistletoe?"

As a matter of fact, I ran into a foxhunter from the Brandywine Hunt several years later. He told me he had looked at Mistletoe's game leg at the horse dealers' place and decided Mistletoe would come sound with a little time off. Sure enough, she did and he hunted her for a couple of years. He also got a nice colt and dandy little filly out of Mistletoe. It was a lucky day for him when I decided to sell Mistletoe.

I lied shamelessly, saying, "Well, I got a horse with a little more foot than old Mistletoe."

The reader may well think that I acted like a bloody fool. The honest answer is that whenever I think of Mistletoe, I know I did.

THE GREAT MARCH FOX HUNT

We few, we happy few . . .
SHAKESPEARE, RICHARD V

On the first Saturday in March, 1968, the Vicmead Hunt had enjoyed its best Saturday hunt since Thanksgiving. A large dog (male) fox had taken us from the Millpond all the way to Malmo Farm and back. He had given us a very fast hour and a half all around Malmo Farm as well as the Caldwell place. However, when Friday, March 7, rolled around, upper New Castle County was covered with about an inch of soft, wet snow. It seemed virtually certain that there would be no foxhunting down in Middletown the next day. But Friday turned unexpectedly warm: a good deal of the snow melted. I telephoned the Vicmead Huntsman, Oscar Crossan, around 7:00 a.m. Saturday morning and hesitatingly inquired, "Any chance that we are going out today?"

Oscar replied a trifle gruffly, "Well, as you know, the Master, Mrs. Carpenter, is away, but I am going to try it. But remember, there is more snow predicted for this afternoon."

I was keeping my horse, Tug, at home. I cleaned Tug, and fed him a solid ration of Red Rose Super Horse Feed. I put in a call to Rowe. I said excitedly, "Hot dog, Rowe! Hounds are going out. Can you pick Tug up?"

Rowe replied, "Now, have I ever let you down, Billy Boy? Of course, I'll be there at your place at 10:30 sharp. Have Tug good and ready, Lad, and we'll be off for a good day of hunting." Rowe was in his early sixties and, although a beautiful rider, had entirely given up foxhunting himself. He, however, seemed to take vicarious pleasure in my hunting.

After a light breakfast of cereal, I got to the office at about 8:00 a.m. with my hunting clothes and boots under my Saturday working clothes (grey flannels and a sport coat).

At 11:15, I said good-bye to my father and cleared out of the office on the dead

Vicmead hounds, about 1965. Photographer: Unknown.

run, a dozen pressing matters still not taken care of. My father tacitly approved of my fox-hunting: actually, I am sure he was envious of my Saturdays in the saddle. I drove at breakneck speed down familiar roads to Middletown so as to be there punctually at noon sharp, the Saturday meeting time of the Vicmead.

The winter day was gray and somewhat overcast but not too cold. To the west, large snow clouds were piling up. The meet was near Bayard Sharp's house. As I drove in the long lane, there were ponies of all kinds, sizes and shapes streaming in from all directions since Lana Wright's Middletown Pony Club had been invited to join the hunt that day. Ten couples (in foxhunting parlance twenty hounds) were grouped on the front lawn of Bayard's house around Oscar's horse under the watchful eyes of the two whips, Chappie Fraser and Oscar's son, Monk Crossan. Vicmead's Master of Foxhounds, Merton Carpenter, had asked Harry Mechling to act as Field Master that day since she was going to be in Florida. Harry's duties would be purely nominal (keeping the field well back of Oscar, who, as we all well knew, threw a tantrum if any member of the field dared to get in his way or crowded him or his hounds). Of course, the successful hunting of a pack of hounds is a delicate and difficult task and requires the full and undivided attention of the Huntsman. Rowe O'Neal had once said to me, "It don't make no difference how good a pack of hounds is. The results depend on how good and knowledgeable the Huntsman really is." Good whips operate as an extension of the Huntsman as well as additional eyes and ears. The Field Master's job is to keep the field out of the way but close enough to be able to see and enjoy the hounds work.

I quickly got out of my car and stripped off my flannels, my sport coat and my tie. I tucked my shirt collar inside my shirt and wrapped a frayed stock around my neck, knotted it, and pinned it with a diaper pin borrowed from my infant daughter, Annie. In spite of repeated and patient lessons over the past years, I had not (and still have not) mastered the real knack of tying a stock properly, especially in a car mirror with my eager horse milling around, impatient to be off and away. Rowe had led my heavy halfbred horse, Tug, out of his van, stripped off his blanket and halter, tightened the girth and pulled both stirrups smartly down with a snap. He held Tug steady while I put my left foot in the iron (stirrup) and swung up and into the saddle. As I trotted away, Rowe called out, "Good hunting!" I knew he would follow the hunt all afternoon in my car, with his buddy, Smitty, a fellow van man. I joined Oscar and the small field just as he got ready to blow his horn and move off.

There were a fair number of Pony Clubbers out but the only other Vicmead members besides myself were Harry Mechling, Bob Peoples, and Lana Wright. All the dozen to eighteen regulars were away or thought the hounds would not go out because of the threatening weather.

Oscar blew his horn and the hounds moved off. It was just noon and we were starting right on time. There were some patches of snow on the shady sides of the woods. The ground was soft; the going would be heavy, particularly in muddy fields. Sawmill Woods was hunted without success. However, in the fields on the far side, one of the

Oscar Crossan, Huntsman, Vicmead Hunt Club, about 1965. Photographer: Unknown.

hounds opened (sang out) dubiously on what was obviously the stale line of a fox who had been this way a long, long time before. The hounds hunted this line fitfully for a couple of fields or so, but the little leftover scent soon petered out. Oscar then decisively picked up his hounds and moved briskly back towards the woods lying across the Choptank Road to the west. As we went over a three-rail fence and into the back part of Bayard Sharp's farm, Monk's horse slid on some greasy mud and Monk came off. Though neither he nor his horse was any the worse for the fall, it obviously wasn't going to be much of a day for jumping. He muttered angrily at his horse as it was brought back to him by his fellow whip, Chappie Fraser. Monk put his foot back in the stirrup, vaulted lightly back into the saddle, cracked his whip at a laggard hound and galloped off. Incidentally, Monk, like all good whips, never actually used his whip on a hound. The most he would do was to just touch a miscreant hound very lightly and expertly with the red linen thong on the very end of his long leather whip. Usually all he had to do was to swing his long whip expertly around his head and then sharply crack the whip, making a sound like a pistol shot.

We hunted westward down these woods for a mile or so. Oscar then circled the pack to the left and cast his hounds (directed the hounds by voice commands and gestures) into a tiny bit of covert full of disgraceful trash: bed springs, a tractor tire, rusty wire, beer cans, broken bottles, a wrecked car, a T.V. with its guts hanging out and several old white refrigerators. I could not imagine why he was wasting time by drawing (having his hounds hunt) this small bit of scrub trees, undergrowth and trash. Oscar obviously suspected that there just might be a fox there. By golly, he was right! Quite suddenly we had a momentary view of a small gray fox who came darting out of the covert. He then popped right back in again. There followed the usual pandemonium that ensues due to the fact that our native gray fox rarely leaves his den area to run cross country (as the red fox does), preferring to mill about his home covert for a bit before going down a hole. The hounds were running wildly around every which way through the cover, all excited and all giving tongue (baying). Every once in a while there would be a fleeting glimpse of our gray fox.

Finally, to everyone's surprise, Chappie hallooed: he had viewed the gray fox sneaking out of the covert which was now full of hounds running all around in different directions. Smiles lit up the faces of the Pony Clubbers and the small field. But after a couple of fields, the gray fox turned back east and was viewed again, first stealthily skirting the edge of the covert from which he had come and then going right back into the covert again. Oscar, with the help of the whips, recalled his hounds. They were put into the covert again but the gray was nowhere to be found. This gray fox had certainly gone to earth in the safety of some convenient hole. (No loss, as you will soon see.) It was then about 1:30 p.m.

Oscar again picked up his hounds. The pack trotted obediently at his heels down the lane lying alongside Vicmead's kennels. At about this time, we lost all but two of the most determined Pony Clubbers. The others had had a little action and the going had been very heavy: they had had enough.

As he went by us, Oscar said he thought we would do better because scent now seemed good and was getting better all the time. Oscar then cast his hounds again. The hounds went gaily into a covert back of the kennels. Harry Mechling, Bob Peoples and I followed Oscar and the whips towards the south side of the covert overlooking the Great Bohemia Creek. The two remaining Pony Clubbers and Lana were a little way behind us. As we walked slowly along the south side of the covert towards the bottom, we were about fifty feet behind Oscar. Then all of a sudden, the notes from his copper horn changed abruptly from an occasional encouraging call to his hounds to the urgent and staccato notes of "Gone away!" These blasts on the horn signalled the hounds and the field (and indeed the fox) that a fox had been viewed. Up to that moment, not a single hound had opened. Only Oscar himself had viewed our new fox. But, indeed, there right in front of us and just coming out of the covert was one of the biggest dog foxes that I had ever seen. He was fully a yard long from the tip of his very shiny little nose to the tip of his long bushy tail tipped with a tiny white spot. He was strawberry blond in color. This fox was running easily but swiftly about 75 yards away from us in an easterly direction. When he had gone about another 150 yards, he stopped and looked back. Three hounds had come out of the covert. The fox quickly got up and quietly disappeared over the brow of the hill followed by the three lead hounds. From the covert came the sound of the cracking of whips as Monk and Chappie tried to encourage the rest of the pack to get on the line.

Some of the hounds opened and soon all the rest were in full cry but going in the wrong direction. We thought that they were running "heel" (running the fox's line backward—that is, in the direction from which the fox had come). But Harry Mechling said, "I viewed the vixen quietly going out the other side of the covert. Maybe it was her line the hounds were following."

Bob Peoples added, "Now is the time of year that dog foxes go courting. This just might be a visiting fox." Finally, with the help of the whips, Monk and Chappie, all the hounds were put on the line of the dog fox and going the right way. They were soon all running flat out on the line of the fox following their three early brothers. We were now off on the Great March Fox Hunt.

Once the hounds had streamed by, they were followed by Oscar, the two whips, Harry Mechling, Lana Wright, Bob Peoples, myself and the two hardy remnants of the Pony Club. After disappearing over the low hill, the fox turned right handed and went down towards the Great Bohemia Creek. The hounds followed the fox's line after a momentary check after which Oscar cast the pack in a widening circle. They then pushed on through the small pine woods. We followed at a brisk canter. We all thought this might well have been the same fox that we had hunted the week before. Bob and I whooped with excitement like school boys playing hookey as we galloped along.

Harry sang out, "Guys, it looks like we are going to go all the way to Malmo Farm again today."

I could not help shouting, "Hooray! Hooray!"

However, this time, our fox took us on up through the heavy plowed fields on the left side of the Millpond. He then turned sharp right and went across the deep stream that feeds the Millpond, went on through the woods and came out in the fields lying just to the west of Jesse Unruh's farm. We followed on down the small hill, over an "in and out" (a pair of fences set 10 to 15 yards apart), splashed through the stream and galloped up the other side. Our fox now led us down across Bunker Hill Road. I hoped that he would go back and into the Cherry Tree country but he had now headed generally back in the direction of the Great Bohemia Creek. I thought to myself that once there he would almost certainly seek the safety of a familiar earth after this brisk run.

However, this fox had a mind of his own. My fears were clearly not his. Spurning a quick return to the safety of an earth in the area where he had started, this bold fox crossed the marshes just below the Millpond. To our surprise and delight, he then went flying to the west down towards the Middleneck Peninsula which lies between and is bounded by the Greater Bohemia and Little Bohemia Creeks. Oscar's hounds were working together beautifully under his guidance—all together except for two nine-year old bitches who were unable to keep up when scent was hot but who led the pack when scenting became tougher and the rest of the pack was at a temporary loss. In the plowed fields, the going was very heavy: horses sank almost to their hocks (horses' legs below the knees). I could feel the energy draining out of even muscular Tug as he struggled gamely across still another muddy field.

Oscar Crossan, Huntsman, and Harry Mechling.
Photographer: Unknown.

Our fox was indeed headed toward the Middleneck. We followed, crossing the bridge on the top of the Millpond Dam and then on to a small path lying back of the newly built house at the top of the little hill. We could hear the hounds but could not see them because they were now well on ahead of us in the woods. The ground was lightly covered with melting snow. Oscar, who was directly ahead of us on the small path still covered with snow, did not even pause at a stout three-rail fence set at a crazy angle: he jumped it catty-corner. Neither did Bob nor Harry nor I pause: we also sailed on over. The whips were on ahead. We galloped on a new path across to the woods, popped over a "chicken coop" (a triangular sort of fence) on the far side, clambered up a short steep bank and on into the broad brown fields that marked the real beginning of Middleneck. Oscar paused there momentarily, uncertain whether this dog fox was really serious about going down the Middleneck or was about to swing around, elude the hounds and go back to his home in the covert which lay behind us directly on the other side of the Greater

Bohemia. The diminishing sounds of the hounds soon left no doubt that our fox was indeed serious about going on down the Middleneck. Oscar, then the whips, Chappie and Monk, and Harry Mechling, Bob Peoples and I were all that was left at this point: the Pony Clubbers had had quite enough, thank you. Lana Wright, of course, could have out-stayed all of us, but she loyally saw that all of her young charges got safely home. We were careful to gallop on the very edges of the fields, but still our horses sank down in the soft March mud. A three-rail fence capped our crossing of these muddy fields. All of the horses somehow scrambled over this fence. Monk's horse, however, turned for some reason at the very last moment and went up over the post (safely, thank goodness).

We galloped on down to the farm and opened a high cattle gate since the Middleneck country had never been opened (fenced) for foxhunting. Thus, the country was impassable in places for horses, though not for hounds nor, of course, for our hard running fox. It was about a mile down the farm road to the hard road. The going on the dirt road was good. Our horses were refreshed even though they were now going at full gallop. At the end of the farm road there was an iron cattle guard (a series of parallel iron bars set in the road to keep the cattle in). All of our horses somehow managed to get across the cattle guard. We then turned right handed and went pounding down the road that leads west to the very end of the Middleneck. Over to our right and parallel to us, we could hear and, at times, see our hard working hounds pushing along in and out of the woods or disappearing behind the low hills and coming in sight again as they came on out of the swales.

Because of the March wind, we could not always hear the distant sound of the cry of the hounds as they pushed farther and farther west. We then came across several American hounds looking lost and forlorn; we figured they were from old Walter Drummond's pack since he and his buddies often hunted this very same country in his old red International pickup truck.

Finally, we got to a place beyond which I, at least, had never gone. Always before, foxes had turned around and come across the road and then looped back to more familiar country. This time, however, the fox and our pursuing hounds pushed on and on. At one point, the hounds ran through fields where thousands of Canadian geese were feeding. The almost total stillness of the March afternoon was shattered as each goose called to his neighbor as he took to the air. Harry Mechling shouted as we cantered along, "I bet that there are 5,000 geese in that field!" The hounds went right on by them, paying no attention whatsoever to this feathery distraction.

At last, at the very end of the point of land, we came in sight of the tall chimneys of the large white house, Little Bohemia. Since we were going by way of the road, we got to the lawn of the house itself before the hounds. No one seemed to be home. We could hear the hounds pushing the fox along through the underbrush that lies on the very edge of the Greater Bohemia. This was our first, last and only real check. It gave our white lathered horses some chance to dry off a bit, rest up and drink from the muddy puddles left by the melting snow. My ragged stock, my button-down shirt, my old yellow wool vest and even my heavy hunting coat were all drenched with sweat in spite of the somewhat brisk winter weather. Soon, however, Tug was pulling, jigging and snorting: he at least was eager to be off again. Oscar sat there watching his hounds work the fox's line without his guidance.

We sat on our horses on the lawn of the big house. The view was magnificent. The lawns and brown fields sloped gently down to the icy water on three sides. On one side lay Great Bohemia Creek. It was now the size of a river and flowed in and out under the bridge, depending on the tide. On the left was the Little Bohemia, hardly smaller. They joined in front of us to form a bay that flowed on out into the Chesapeake. Shafts of late afternoon sunlight pierced the menacing winter clouds. Great flocks of Canadian geese in vee formations wheeled around high overhead making their regular late afternoon flight, honking to one another. Swift smaller squadrons of mallards, black ducks and others sped this way and that across the late afternoon sky. Way around to the left we could just see the white octagonal bell tower rising from the square brick steeple of the Old Bohemia Church built by the Jesuits in 1704. In answer to my question, Harry said, "Charles Carroll, a signer of the Declaration of Independence, went to school at Bohemia Academy, also built by the Jesuits in 1754, as did his brother, Thomas Carroll, the first Catholic Bishop in America." We drank in this view. I stored it to savor with pleasure for dark days and nights sure to come in the years ahead.

I weakened and smoked a cigarette. I silently hoped and then said aloud, "I pray that our fox will double this point and lead us back along the very edge of the Little Bohemia." No sooner had I said these words than our hopes were realized. After several checks, to our surprise and delight, the hounds pushed out into the fields that lie between the house and the edge of the Little Bohemia. Thus, our hounds were continuing their run in a great sweeping counterclockwise circle, reaching to the very end of the point of land to the west. Now, they had begun going back eastward again through the waist-high brown weeds. The fox had obviously been that way: our hounds were having a little trouble with scent but were pushing on hard, finding, losing, finding again, and speaking when they caught the scent of our fox. It was now well past 4:00. We had been running this fox for well over two and a half hours.

Harry exclaimed ruefully, "My gosh, we have house guests who have come all the way from Virginia. They are coming to celebrate my birthday." He looked at his watch, saying, "I, at this very moment am supposed to be home right now!" Looking across the half mile of water to his house, he sighed, "If the fox would only take to the water, so would I." Harry finally remarked, thinking of his wife, Jo, his birthday dinner and his guests, "It is only half a mile across the water but fourteen miles around." However, the fox, probably unmindful that he was causing Harry a large domestic and social problem, was now moving firmly eastward. The hounds seemed to be gaining on the fox. Bob and I went down to the river and tried to follow the hounds along the banks of the Little Bohemia but, as Oscar warned us, barbed wire fences and marshes effectively frustrated our efforts. At one point, I considered asking Tug to jump a low barbed wire fence to stay up with the hounds but prudently I refrained. (Was I getting older, or wiser?) Those up on the road told me later that they had viewed our fine upstanding fox at about this point jumping boldly through the hedge rows and loping easily over the fields. Finally, both of us came back up on the road.

After riding along the road for a mile or so, we again left the road and went along a hedgerow towards which the hounds were heading. We were now ahead of the hounds, having moved by road. Oscar looked carefully at a patch of snow on the shady side of a bank of honeysuckle. Oscar called us over to where he was peering down to the ground, "Look here. These are the fresh little foot prints of our fox. See, they are altogether different from the big blunt prints that the hounds make." Oscar also wrinkled up his nose and sniffed, saying, "If you have a good sniffer, you can smell the scent of a fox. On a day like this when the scent is good and there is no wind, even us humans can smell the fox." Oscar was right: there was a faint pungent odor somewhat like the faint smell of a skunk. With a few short blasts on his copper horn, Oscar soon had his pack of hounds around him. He then cast them again, now much closer to our dainty-footed fox.

Earlier in the afternoon, as noted, we had come across some of Paul Drummond's hounds on the Middleneck Road. We now came across Paul himself in his pickup truck. Paul said, "A couple of my best hounds got lost. Keep an eye out for them, would ya?" Sure enough, not long afterward, we came across four old American hounds with long ears and sad eyes lumbering along. They were obviously lost and tried to join our hounds. However, these old fellows simply could not keep up with our hard driving English pack. Very soon we could hear these veterans solemnly baying mournfully far to the rear. Oscar scornfully remarked, "There ain't an American hound within two hundred miles that would have amounted to anything on such a run." Bob, Harry and I smiled in agreement.

As we plowed along through the heavy fields behind our hounds, we all knew that the fox was about to face another critical decision: where to go when he came back off the Middleneck. Was he going to swing to the left, cross the road and go back across the Millpond and thence home, or would he keep going straight and into the Cherry Tree country? We did not have long to wait: suddenly, our hounds veered sharp left and went across the Middleneck Road, running back the way they had come down four hours ago. We galloped back down the hard road, over the cattle guard and down the long farm lane, back over the fences, over the heavy fields, down the hill and across the chicken coop. At the dam of the Millpond, we could see our pack of still determined hounds streaming across the marshes and the stream. Soon they were on the other side and were going back up into the lower woods. We were sure that the fox would now go back home for a well earned rest. We therefore went up the road and over into the heavy plowed fields. We were now back at the covert where our fox had started hours ago. As we came on up, the shadows had perceptibly lengthened and the pale winter sun sank behind the bank of grey clouds. The temperature had dropped perceptively.

As I said, we all fully expected that the fox would go to his cozy den and rest from the heroic run that he had put on. Perhaps he would rejoin his vixen. Not at all: the fox came right through the woods and turned east. Then, he went down into the covert close to the river and then turned north and came flying up and went into the pine woods lying below the Vicmead kennels. The hounds sailed on through the pine woods. We galloped behind, trying not to slip on the snowy pine needles and muddy places on the south side. The afternoon shadows were lengthening. The hounds, however, were still pressing forward. Oscar's horn kept blowing "Gone away."

Far to the right of us, we could hear the hounds in the kennels who, hearing the excitement, were raising a terrific din. We passed the new barns which had been built on the property that had belonged to the Vicmead. Ahead of us in the pine grove lying to the west of the kennel property, the hounds were at first at fault but then came across the Stagecoach Road. There was Rowe who had been following by car with professional interest and mounting excitement all afternoon. He pointed out exactly where the fox had crossed. Rowe shouted as I galloped on by, "That sure is one fine fox."

The hounds were soon on again. They swung right behind the ancient Mason-Dixon marker, with the arms of William Penn on the Delaware side and those of the Carrolls on the Maryland side, which marks the boundary between Maryland and Delaware. Then we went on down through the woods and over a little coop. Soon we were again plowing across the fields that we covered five hours ago while chasing the timid gray fox. The pale sun had entirely gone down behind the threatening gray clouds in the west. It had gotten much, much colder.

By now, it was well past 6:00 p.m. and getting dark. It was becoming more and more difficult to see the hounds ahead. However, we went down into the woods and over the in and out, across the stream and up right handed on the side of the Millpond stream. Ahead of us, hounds were still in full cry and seemed to be gaining on our fox. Harry, at a check, said quietly, "Notice that Oscar isn't pushing his hounds so hard now—like every Huntsman, he would like to account for this fox (put him to earth), but he sure doesn't want to catch and kill this great fox, and neither do I." Bob and I agreed.

We went down in the woods. There ahead of us in the gathering gloom was the large wooden gate which had resulted in so many nasty falls over the years. As we stood still there for a momentary check, I said to Bob Peoples that once the hounds moved out again we were going to have to jump that awful gate in total darkness. Bob Peoples replied, "Not me and not you, if you have any sense."

Wiser heads prevailed: before the hounds moved off again, the grisly gate was opened by Monk, at his father's prudent direction. The five of us cantered gratefully and safely through. Crossing the road, we went into Fox Park, passing the place where the Thanksgiving fox, certainly a relative of the present fox, had unfortunately been "rolled over" after a glorious run of an hour and a half. We moved out of the woods on the far side. By now, the evening gloom had given way to frank darkness. The only thing that could be seen were the twinkling lights of the farmhouses and barns in the country around us, the patches of white snow and our own horses' heads. The hounds could, however, still be heard pressing northward and probably, at last, headed towards Malmo Farm.

It was now quarter of seven and time to call a halt, even though the fox didn't seem to know it. Tug seemed eager to go on, though the day had been long, the going heavy with a substantial number of serious fences. Our hounds were still gay and aggressive.

Bob said, "We could hunt all night if only there was a friendly moon to light our way." It was with obvious reluctance that Oscar lifted his horn to try to recall his pack of hard driving hounds. By ones and twos the hounds finally came back to him through the evening darkness, wagging their sterns as Oscar called each by name and praised them individually. When the last little bitch hound had come back, Oscar blew the call that signals the end of a day's hunting. Oscar turned his horse's head towards the kennels. Through the darkness the pack closely followed on his horse's heels. No need for Monk and Chappie to crack their whips. It was only then that we realized that, not only were our horses dead tired but we, ourselves, had been going steadily since noon, almost seven hours ago. Our horses had occasionally had a drink from a muddy puddle or a stream but it had been a long, long time since my light breakfast of cereal and coffee. At 7:30, we finally got back to Bayard Sharp's house, dismounted stiffly, blanketed and loaded our horses in vans for their trip home and a well earned rest. It began to snow.

I went over to Oscar, his son, Monk, and Chappie and complimented them for a truly memorable day of foxhunting.

Oscar gruffly acknowledged that it had been a good day and added, "It don't take no skill to hunt these hounds with such good scent and such a fine fox. I only hope we'll be able to find and hunt him many a day. Well, good night to the three of you."

I turned to Harry and said, "Happy Birthday, Harry. I bet today's hunt is a birthday present you'll never forget. I know I never will!" And I never have.

This, then, is the story of the Great March Fox Hunt: that's how it was!

You may have noticed that the Thanksgiving Fox got rolled over (was killed). The explanation of how that happened is as follows. The Thanksgiving Fox could, if he had chosen, not come out of his hole that day. Also, he could have popped right back down his own hole or gone in another hole when he first heard the Huntsman's horn or the baying of the hounds. The death of the Thanksgiving fox was a total accident. The fox was turned by an old farmer and his grandson who were walking off their Thanksgiving dinner. John Tabbett, the old farmer, was himself a coon hound hunter. He knew exactly what had happened and why, and he felt terrible about it. For years afterward, John would stop and explain to anyone who would listen to him that turning the fox was the last thing in the world he and his grandson wanted to do or intended to do.

Oscar also felt badly about the death of the Thanksgiving Fox. He had tried his best to stop his hounds when he saw that the fox had been turned. But, as Oscar explained, "There is almost no way a Huntsman can stop a pack of hounds running hard on a line of good scent and about to close in a fox."

FANNY'S LAST POINT-TO-POINT

To finish is to win.
MOTTO – AMERICAN ENDURANCE RIDE CONFERENCE

Recently, I was in my law office talking on the telephone when the morning mail was brought in. I received the usual dull stuff, bills, a deluge of legal papers, letters and notices. But I saw among the rest the calendar of spring timber racing events in the *Chronicle of the Horse* or some similar horse magazine. I read it avidly. The droning voice of my caller faded as a cascade of a thousand memories and bright images flashed across my mind. I was lost thinking back to racing weekends of the past, glorious windy March days and rain drenched Saturdays in April, the exhilaration of the first hint of an impending romance and the twinge of remembered bitterness of seeing an old flame five years after it was all over, the tweedy parents of college friends and the charming Christopher Robins of the same college friends, monumental hangovers, and the endless drives back to college or home on Sundays. As my caller droned on and on, I ran down the familiar list of spring races, the Manor Race, the Blockhouse Race, and the Maryland Hunt Cup. Eventually, my eyes came to rest on the Radnor Spring Races. Instantly, I felt butterflies in my stomach and my hands went clammy. They always do when I think about the Radnor Races. That is somewhat the point of this account.

This account would be more accurately titled "Fanny's First Point-to-Point." The actual title makes it sound as if Fanny and I raced many, many times and this account is written on the occasion of my hanging up my racing tack and Fanny being retired after a string of brilliant victories over timber (fences made of timber rails as contrasted with fences made of brush). In truth, the race in question was not only my first but also my last point-to-point, and it was also Fanny's first and last effort over timber, at least as long as I had her. Let me first describe Fanny and then go on to explain how I got us into this particular situation.

Fanny on loan from Peter Winants, 1957-1963. Photographer: Unknown.

Fanny on loan from Peter Winants, 1957-1963. Photographer: Unknown.

Fanny, as the name implies, was a mare. She was bred from a race horse stallion and a brood mare. Janon Fisher bred her for Peter Winants who at the time weighed in at better than 210 pounds. He needed a horse with stamina and jumping ability to carry him over the fields, hills and fences of the Elkridge-Harford and Greenspring hunting country in Maryland. From the time she was a filly, Fanny had the likeable disposition of her gentle mother but the fire of her timber stallion father. She was a large horse with great shoulders, bulging quarters, and pie plate feet. Fanny, it must be confessed, had a distinctly Roman nose. Her color was unique: a soft brown liver color. She was covered with beautiful dapples. But this brief description does not do Fanny justice. Certainly, she was not a thoroughbred, but she was very handsome in her own way and perfectly fitted for the job of a hunting mare. Fanny loved hunting and jumping. Yet she was so gentle and so quiet that ladies and even small children could and did hunt her.

Fanny, having been thoroughly broken and admirably schooled, had been hunted for a single season. Unfortunately my friend, Peter Winants, Fanny's owner, felt he had to give up hunting for at least a year. He called me in August 1960 and asked if I would be interested in hunting Fanny for a season or two. I agreed immediately. Not only was I between horses, but I have a policy of never looking gift horses in the mouth.

I called Rowe O'Neal. As the reader knows, he was my mentor in all matters having to do with horses. I told Rowe of my good fortune. He had a professional Irish horseman's skepticism when it came to horses and especially hunting horses being loaned as gift horses, so to speak. Rowe said very little, but I could tell that he was reserving judgment as to the true extent of my good fortune. All he said was, "I can go down to Maryland and van this here mare back in a day or so."

Rowe told me later that when he saw Fanny's huge proportions and her Roman nose and huge feet, he wondered if I was being lent a plow or cart horse rather than a hunting mare. However, he later reported, "But there was just something in the way the mare handled herself in getting into my van that gave me some suspicions that my doubts were all wrong." It was late at night before Rowe got back to his house and neat little white barn at Red Lion, Pennsylvania. The moon had come up. He said, "I couldn't resist clapping a saddle on that big mare. I pointed Fanny at one of the three-rail schooling fences in my front pasture. Before she went over that first fence, I knew that Fanny was indeed a true hunting mare. Still, I was surprised because she was fat and full of summer grass, and she had no shoes on. But, Fanny galloped eagerly in the pale August moonlight towards that strange jump, stood well back and went right over it. That one jump told me right then and there that you were one lucky fellow and in for a great hunting season."

Since I was busy with my practice, I decided not to bring Fanny over to my place at Corner Ketch. I asked Rowe if he could board Fanny for me. Now, he was always buying and selling horses. Horses passed through his four-stall barn on an almost daily basis. Rowe earlier had explained, "Boarding is nothing but a headache and a nuisance." Fortunately Rowe had, already taken a fancy to the big liver-colored mare. To my surprise, he said, "Sure, I'll keep Fanny for you."

The arrangement worked well. Fanny would hang her big neck over the stall door and stamp her feet early in the morning, eager for Rowe's arrival and her double ration of golden oats. I occasionally went over and exercised her, but Bea Crossan, Rowe's friend and neighbor whose riding confidence had been shaken by a series of nasty falls, also took a liking to Fanny. Thus, Bea restored her nerve by galloping Fanny across the Pennsylvania countryside and occasionally popping over one of the many chicken coops or three-rail fences that abound in that part of the world. On Saturdays, Rowe loaded Fanny in his big blue van. I dashed down from the law office to meet the van and Rowe and Fanny at noon at the Vicmead meet near Middletown. Usually, I was just finishing changing into hunting clothes as Oscar Crossan, the Vicmead Huntsman, cheerily blew his horn. Then the mare and I were off for a day of foxhunting. Often Bea would come down with Rowe. I sensed that it was with some slight reluctance that both Rowe and Bea saw an ungainly rider swing heavily into the saddle astride their beloved Fanny.

Fanny was an excellent hunting mare. She loved hunting and everything to do with it. She knew instinctively when Saturdays rolled around and pawed in her stable and gave an occasional neigh. Out hunting, she was always pushing boldly to the front, eager to be the first horse over the fences after the Huntsman, the whips and the Master, and away with the hounds who were already streaming over the next hill. At a check, she again pawed and stamped her big feet as if impatient to push the hounds onward, or as if she herself wanted to go into the covert and push the fox out so that she could go on galloping and jump and jump again. She was very handy for all of her huge size. Fanny had some foot and could and would go all day long and, I suppose, all night if need be.

Fences were her delight and her specialty. She liked them high and handsome and often. When Fanny caught sight of a fence, her stride lengthened a notch or two and her ears perked up with obvious eagerness as she gathered her large body for a clean jump over the fence, her great shoulder muscles bulging and her neck arching. Her distinguished Roman nose became a familiar sight at the Vicmead on Saturdays. She quickly became a favorite with everyone. But, Rowe (and Bea, when she was there) were especially pleased when Fanny was safely returned to them. I think they were somewhat relieved to find each time that she had come home safely: I don't think they cared much one way or another about the rider; after all, there were plenty of riders, but there was only one Fanny.

The first, but not the last, falling out I had with Rowe was when I lent Fanny to a visitor from Virginia who happened to need a horse to hunt. Rowe, though he was tolerant and allowed me to ride Fanny, was not at all happy that Fanny was being loaned to a stranger. Rowe grumbled, "An accident could happen. Then you'd be forever without the services of Fanny. What then? Think about that before you lend her here and there." The visitor was an accomplished foxhunter and indeed a race rider. Not unexpectedly, she rolled her large brown eyes when Fanny marched ponderously out of the Rowe's van. However, after a brilliant day with the Vicmead, she, like everyone else, became a member of Fanny's fan club. It was then that I realized the true situation: though I had the temporary loan of Fanny through the continued generosity of Peter Winants, actually, Rowe (and Bea) had come to regard themselves the true owners of Fanny. I was only being allowed to ride her by their sufferance on Saturdays.

Toward the end of each summer, I dutifully telephoned Peter and asked as casually as I could, "By the way, I hope you are going to be able to hunt this upcoming season."

Year after year, Peter replied, "Doggone it, I am too gosh durn busy. I'll have to put off hunting for yet another season. You will be doing me a favor by hunting Fanny for another season."

I think I can quite honestly say that I really hoped with each call that Peter would say that he was going to start hunting again. After all, there were other good horses in the world, but Peter, like the rest of us, only had so many hunting seasons. Of course, I was only human, so I was overjoyed each time Peter consigned Fanny to me for another glorious foxhunting season. I never told Rowe of these annual inquiries since he obviously saw the mare as a permanent fixture in his stable. It would have needlessly troubled him if he had known of my annual inquiry as to whether the mare would be mine, or rather his, for yet another season. Year after year, Fanny had the choice corner stall in Rowe's well appointed barn, and Peter Winants received a case of good Maryland Rye at Christmas.

It's time or past time to come to the point of this account. There came a year when the Vicmead Hunt Club was invited to mount a three-man hunt team in the spring hunt team race. This meant little or nothing to me. I had gone for years to the spring race meets and had enjoyed the vicarious excitement of these timber races with only an occasional "Walter Mitty" reverie. I had never really thought of actually participating in a timber race. Indeed, in this very year, I had absolutely no thought of participating. Three younger and far more able riders with sleek, trim thoroughbred hunters were eagerly looking forward to the end of winter and the beginning of spring racing, including this particular race. Rowe, Fanny and I were looking forward to one or two more sloppy Saturdays of March hunting in the deep plowed fields with the first sign of spring already showing at the edges of the streams. Then Fanny would be gradually let down until May when she would be turned out for a long and well earned rest in the lush grass of the pasture at my father's place.

Rowe O'Neal. Photographer: Unknown.

That particular winter, the always unwanted snow piled up in February. Fresh onslaughts came early in March. Then, a Vicmead team rider's horse pulled up lame in mid-March. It looked like the Vicmead was not going to field a hunt team. At a hunting meeting, we reviewed the Vicmead's small hunting field to find a replacement, but there simply wasn't any. Having had several stiff "belts," I suddenly heard myself saying, "The honor of the Vicmead must be upheld. Fanny and I will go!" I was instantly incredulous. I knew in my heart of hearts that I had made a big fat mistake, but secretly, I wanted to try timber racing at least once. Everyone was delighted.

One of the race riders said, "Great! Fanny is a real good fencer. She has some foot. I am quite, quite sure that Fanny will be able to get around the Radnor timber course with credit to herself, you and the Vicmead." It was a done deal: Fanny and I would be part of the three-man Vicmead Hunt Team.

The next day at six o'clock in the morning, I surprised Rowe at his early morning chores. I remarked as casually as I could that I'd like to take Fanny out for a little morning gallop. We saddled Fanny up. I took her out and rode briskly over the familiar Pennsylvania countryside, jumping everything in sight. The mare was surprised, but delighted. Usually morning sessions had been more in the nature of birdwatching than skylarking over jumps. During the next week or so, I appeared at Rowe's stable several times as the sun was peeping up over the frosty March hillsides. He said nothing for a while, but I knew Rowe suspected the worst.

Finally, one morning, Rowe turned right around and asked bluntly, "You are taking Fanny in that damned point-to-point, ain't you now?" I said weakly that it was out of my hands and there was nothing I could do. Rowe didn't answer, but I could tell as he turned on his heel that he disapproved with all his Irish heart. However, like so many things, once in motion, this undertaking could not be stopped: I was committed. Even Rowe's grim silence and scowls could not change or alter the swift course of events. I continued the early morning schooling session. My jumping improved somewhat. Fanny didn't need any practice.

Unfortunately, the snow continued late into March. I said to Rowe, "I just think the race might have to be called off." He beamed. It did snow so hard that our team race was first rescheduled to be part of the meet at Fair Hill, Maryland. Then it had to be further rescheduled. The team race was finally moved to the Radnor meet where it was included in the Radnor Race program with a lot of far fancier races. The delay also meant that a lot of other hunts entered the team race, mostly in order to get in a conditioning race in preparation for more serious timber races later in the spring.

"What in the world," I said to myself, "have I gotten myself and dear old Fanny into now?"

Well, finally, the fateful Saturday rolled around. I asked Rowe to van Fanny up. I said, "I'll meet you at Radnor." A curt "Yes, Sir" left no doubt in my mind that my mounting excitement had not permeated his good common sense.

He then blurted out, "This is damned foolishness if you want to know.

William Prickett on Fanny at Team Race, Radnor, 1958. Photographer: Unknown.

You're unnecessarily risking a good mare, and that's all there is to it! And all because you want to show off in a pink coat!" That hurt, perhaps because there was some element of truth in his remark.

I went to the office Saturday morning, as usual. I said casually to my father, "By the way, I am going out riding this afternoon so I might be leaving the office a tad early." No use worrying him unnecessarily. I had borrowed a pink coat and a hunting cap. When I recall the drive up to Radnor, my stomach still has butterflies and my hands go clammy and wet. To this day, my recollection of some of what happened at Radnor has the jewel-like clarity of last night's nightmare.

The winter snows had mostly melted, but the grayish remains of snow drifts on the shady sides of the stone walls and giant rhododendrons had left the turf at Radnor full of water and spongy even on the high ground. The low fields were a sea of mud. I have no memories of lunch with friends in the old Radnor clubhouse. I am certain that I did not feel much like eating anything that day.

The Team Race was the first race on the race card that day. Rowe's florid face was glum as he proudly brought his lovely mare down out of his van. Her mane and tail were neatly braided with Lincoln green wool, Vicmead's color.

A mournful looking Bea Crossan got out of Rowe's van. She laid her hand on my sleeve and implored me, "Please, Bill, for gosh sake, don't take Fanny in this race. Fanny's a hunting horse, not a timber horse!" Bea's voice was breaking and I could see she was close to tears.

"Bea, sorry. There is nothing I can do now. Don't worry yourself. Fanny will take care of herself and me. Just you wait and see."

Bea said worriedly, "Yeah. Well, remember my fall: it took me three years to get over it, and I still ain't right, and they had to put the horse down."

I replied doubtfully, "Really, I didn't know that. See you, Bea."

Rowe led Fanny down into the paddock. When Fanny's green cooler was pulled off, I could see she had been groomed so that each of her dapples glowed. As always, there was a lot of help available. Rowe turned on his heel and marched away with Fanny's halter, blanket and the lead shank without a backward glance. A fellow foxhunter who always rode with shortened stirrups, attesting to his experience as a timber rider, expertly threw the overgirth (a safety measure to make sure the saddle does not slip) over my heavy hunting saddle and pulled it up nice and tight. He then picked up each of Fanny's big front feet in turn to make sure the girth was not pinching her.

Bob Peoples tugged at my sleeve, "Bill, this is just plain crazy. You must scratch Fanny right now." Given a proper excuse, I just might have. But, just then the Radnor Huntsman gave the signal to mount up by a blast on his hunting horn. I was given a leg up into the saddle by Frolic Weymouth.

Once aboard, I leaned down and rechecked the girth as Rowe had taught me. It certainly felt good, as always, to have Fanny under me. The mare was plainly excited but not skittish as we trotted up to the far end of the course away from the clubhouse. The two other Vicmead team riders were experienced race riders. They were each mounted on small, trim timber horses. Indeed, Fanny looked out of place among timber racing

Rowe O'Neal as a member of the Dilwyne Hunt Team with Freddy Pinch and Morris Dixon.
Photographer: Unknown.

horses from Pennsylvania, Maryland, Delaware and even Virginia. Almost everyone else had their stirrups shortened to jockey length, but I kept my stirrups hunting length, mostly because I could not possibly ride, much less jump, with my stirrups shortened. The walking start (a start not out of a starting gate) was a mass of color and confusion since there were 21 horses milling about, all jockeying for position. There was a familiar face or two among the riders, but there was no time for an exchange of greetings. All of a sudden and, for me at least, all too soon, the starter dropped his flag, and the Huntsman blew his horn signaling the start of the race.

All the horses were off in a flash or, at least, all but one of them were. Fanny had been ambling along at the back of the pack going in the opposite direction. It took me a moment to get her turned around. In that instant, the other horses were pounding off at high speed towards the first jump. Fanny set off, immediately realizing that this was a race. She galloped wide open after the other horses. She gained on them and passed one or two horses before the first fence. The first fence was slightly uphill. The welter of horses ahead of us had left the take-off area soft and slippery, but this was nothing new to Fanny. She stood well back and sailed easily and gracefully over this first fence and rolled on, gaining on the other horses. The butterflies were gone. I was literally having the thrill of a lifetime.

After going up a small hill and across a series of fences, Fanny and I came down in the valley. Here the wet weather of the last two weeks was against us. The winter snows and March rains had turned the bottom land into a quagmire. Fanny sank in up to her hocks, but she pounded gamely on across the bottom. Not only was this tiring, but we lost ground to the lighter, smaller and daintier horses who bounced along the top of the muck. This area drained some of Fanny's strength, which would be sorely needed for the ground yet to be covered and the fences yet to be cleared. Still, we had only two miles or so to go. Fanny was in fine fettle and obviously enjoying herself thoroughly. We jumped the next four fences. Fanny did well, standing back and jumping cleanly as she did in the hunting field. There was nothing terribly high or difficult about these fences. She would have done better except for the heavy going. The distance had now lengthened between ourselves and the pack of pink coats preceding us. They were well ahead of us as we came over the shoulder of the hill and took still another fence.

The pace was considerably faster than even the briskest fox hunt. The fast pace and treacherous muddy going had accounted for two of the lead horses. There was one loose horse careening wildly about at odd angles with stirrups flapping and reins askew. As we came back down across the far side of the course, we again came into heavy going. Fanny was now covered with white lather and was breathing heavily. There were only three jumps to go. The leaders were just sweeping up the long hill and finishing to a great hurrah from the crowd at the Radnor clubhouse. We cleared two of the last three jumps.

Fanny was bushed as we came down the long hill. There was still one more piece of bottom land to cross before going over a hard road and then over the final fence. She was still game. However, the last piece of soggy bottom land took away just about all of her remaining strength. After crossing the field, we came across the hard road. Fanny saw the last jump on the far side.

I remember Rowe standing there waving his arms and shouting, "Don't jump!" Bea was with him, her hands covering her eyes. But I wanted to finish and I was dead sure, so to speak, that Fanny could find enough strength to clear this last fence. As always, Fanny's ears perked up and her stride lengthened. However, I felt her hesitate just a tad a couple of strides before that last jump. I kicked her in the flanks. I could feel Fanny gather herself for this one final effort. Too bad, the going had been just too tough. She just could not quite clear that top rail. Both of us cartwheeled head over heels over the fence.

I saw stars for a minute and then began to try to pick myself up, only to be pushed back down again by my friends certain that I must have been hurt in this spectacular fall. I looked around and saw someone sitting on Fanny's head in order to keep her down. Rowe came running over as fast as he could go, followed by Bea. He squatted down, checking Fanny over.

Bea was on her knees beside Fanny, crooning, "Poor old girl. I pray to the good Lord that you're okay. That sure was one terrible fall. Kind of like the spill where I got hurt."

Rowe said nothing: he had Fanny's giant halter over his arm and the shank on ready to lead her back to his van. Just then, two other Vicmead riders came running lickety split down the hill from the finish line.

One shouted as he came, "Bill! Bill! Remount and finish. Then Vicmead will be 4th! Here, let me give you a leg up."

Rowe stood up, whirled around and shouted, his face now purple with anger, "Ain't this mare done enough already for the bloody Vicmead! What's the Vicmead ever done for Fanny, tell me that!"

Bea was in tears and said, "Come on, Bill. Be a good guy and let Rowe and me take Fanny on home and take care of her."

However, Fanny settled the matter for all of us. She suddenly got up on her feet and began to paw and stamp her feet. She gave a large neigh and shook herself all over. Everyone laughed. The one Vicmead rider protested, saying, "Oh, come on now! That's sort of overdoing it, isn't it? Who cares! Let Fanny and Bill go. They've done themselves proud already."

But the other rider pressed, saying that all Fanny had to do was cross the finish line and then Vicmead would be 4th, or maybe even 3rd, if there was a disqualification. "Come on, now, Bill. You're okay, aren't you? I am sure Fanny is okay."

My borrowed pink coat was covered with wet brown mud as were my boots and white pants. I got a leg up again. Fanny, apparently unhurt but covered with white sweat and brown mud, trotted easily up the Radnor lawn and crossed the finish line to the good natured cheers of the few people still there who had not gone down to the paddock to watch the saddling up for the next race.

I hunted Fanny for a couple of more years. Then there came a time when Peter Winants was able to hunt again. I had the sad job of asking Rowe. "Rowe, I hate to tell you and Bea, but Peter Winants is going to hunt again this fall. Can you van her down to Maryland this week?"

Rowe was staggered and finally replied weakly, "I don't believe it! This will kill Bea." Nevertheless, what had to be, had to be.

Peter Winants hunted Fanny and even ran her in heavyweight timber races. Peter, who had heard how fond we all were of the mare, bred Fanny. Her first colt, Tug, was offered to me. I, as always, accepted with alacrity. Of course, Rowe went down to Maryland with Bea the very same day that I told him about Fanny's colt. When they got back, Rowe called me, and said "Bill, you won't believe it, but that colt, Tug, is the spitting image of Fanny. Of course, it will take me a couple of years to turn Tug into a hunting horse, but I am sure that him is going to be just as great a horse as his dam, Fanny, is. I will be plumb tickled to have Fanny's colt right in my own stable. Seems like the good old days!"

CLIPPING

If it ain't broke, don't fix it.
ANONYMOUS

The first horse I got was a good Morgan mare I named Mistletoe. I was a very young, impecunious lawyer, so I acquired an old wooden two-car garage and moved it over to my father's place and turned it into a little stable for Mistletoe. I kept her there.

I didn't know the first thing about caring for a horse. One of my first mistakes was to be too sympathetic in matters of feed. I consistently overfed Mistletoe (and indeed myself). Thus, after a hard day of hunting on Saturdays, I gave her a hot mash Saturday night. That was okay, but then on Sunday, I would give her a double ration of grain or corn or, even worse, sweet feed. One Sunday afternoon, while nursing a monstrous hangover and reading the Sunday *New York Times*, I idly happened to look out the window. To my horror, Mistletoe appeared totally crippled. She was barely able to walk. I thought she was a goner. I called the veterinarian, old Dr. Arnold, right away. He lived on the Old Brick Church Road near Five Corners outside Kennett Square. I told him what the problem was. He knew in a flash what had happened. He said, "For goodness sakes, Son, keep that mare moving. Do not let her lie down! I will be right over."

Dr. Arnold came right on over and examined Mistletoe and promptly gave her a giant shot in her neck. Having taken the necessary steps for her safety, he sternly explained that Mistletoe had what used to be known as "Monday Morning Sickness." He had seen it frequently when he was a young vet in Philadelphia. On cold Monday mornings there would be horses down all over the city because kind stable boys had overfed the draft horses on their Sunday day off. He added, "A diet of grain is just too rich for their kidneys; they tie up."

When I asked what I could do to prevent this from happening again, he replied forcefully, "In the first place, young man, you don't work this horse nearly hard enough.

William Prickett on Liberty. Photographer: James Graham, Montchanin, Delaware.

Before cars, a good horse like yours would be worked hard seven days a week, and they were all the better for it. In fact, hard work is even good for young know-it-all lawyers from Harvard. This horse would haul cans of milk to the freight station every morning; then she'd pull a plow or haul a hay wagon. She'd also pull the family carriage to church on Sundays. She might even hunt some. Now," he glared at me, "all you do is to get up in the morning and give her a fast thirty-minute gallop and then throw her out to pasture. Come Saturday, you hunt her furiously. Then you double feed her on Sunday, 'cuz you feel sorry for her.' It's a wonder she isn't dead already."

His tone softened only slightly as he told me to work her more during the week and hunt her less hard on Saturdays and cut her feed out completely when, probably for reasons of alcohol or sloth, I could not exercise her or myself. He continued, "In other words, give her only hay and plenty of clean water on Sundays, and she'll be fine. I might also prescribe more cold water and less alcohol and beer for you if I weren't just an old horse doctor."

Of course, Dr. Arnold knew what he was talking about. I did exactly as he said as far as Mistletoe was concerned. She never had another episode of tieing up, though I was often tempted by her pleading looks to give her just a little handful of delicious sweet feed on Sundays.

Then, I had another problem from trying to clip Mistletoe.

One fine day when I was out hunting in my first season, Bob Peoples remarked as we were standing at a check, "Mistletoe is looking a little bit furry. You really have to get her clipped."

I asked Rowe O'Neal about clipping as we drove home after the hunt that day. He agreed that Mistletoe needed a hunting haircut and told me he would come over some evening and give her a clip. He said, "Mind you, you will have to keep the mare well blanketed after that as the nights and even the days are getting colder."

Rowe was, of course, as good as his word. One morning later in the week, I came into my little stable and pulled Mistletoe's blanket off. I found that she was smooth and sleek, having been clipped all the way around except for her legs. One winter night, I came on home. There was a light on in the stable. I went on down. There was Rowe, standing on a chair with his little wire spectacles perched right on the end of his red nose. He ran his large horse clippers methodically up and down and sheared off Mistletoe's excess hair. The rope shank attached to her halter was limp. She stood quietly even when Rowe skillfully ran his humming clippers over her head and around her ears. Clipping looked like nothing at all. In Rowe's monthly handwritten bills, prepared by his nice wife, Rose, there would from time to time be an entry "$10—clipping Mistletoe."

Then, one day, I saw Mother clipping her two poodle dogs. I decided that I myself could and would give Mistletoe her next clipping.

Thus, one cold March night, I took a chair down to the stable. I tied Mistletoe's shank to a post. Then, as I had seen Rowe do, I plugged in Mother's poodle clippers to the overhead light and plunged into the work. I took a couple of downward strokes with the clippers and stood back to see the effect. I had not gotten her flank as smooth as I wanted, so I made some strokes at right angles to my initial strokes. Pretty soon there were clipper cuts going all which ways with little tufts sticking up here and there. I decided that I would have to go back over the whole of Mistletoe's left side and clip her again, but all in the same direction. I did so. Then her left side was quite smooth. However, poodle clippers were much finer than Rowe's large horse clippers. The result was that there wasn't a single solitary hair on her left side. Instead, all she had was a sort of five o'clock stubble rising from her pinkish skin. I was aghast at what I had done, but there was no help for it now.

I spent another hour and a half doing exactly the same thing to Mistletoe's other flank. By this time, she was totally naked except for her head, ears, tail and legs. I moved my chair around to the front and approached her head with my whining poodle clippers. Mistletoe pulled back. I knew it had to be done, so I approached her again. She pulled smartly back and then half reared and broke the shank. She clearly did not like the high whining sound that Mother's little poodle clippers made as opposed to Rowe's quiet horse shears. I had to content myself with trying to trim her head with scissors, but this ragged haircut detracted even more from her appearance. What a disaster!

I dreaded what Rowe would say when he saw the carnage I had created. Mistletoe had been a neat looking little mare before I got after her with dog shears. On Saturday morning, I normally went to the office and met Rowe down at the Vicmead meet. However, some times I stayed at the house. That Saturday, I figured I had better be present and face the Irish music. I stayed up at the house. I was fiddling with my stock when I heard Rowe's blue van roll on in. He went briskly, as always, down to my little stable. Then a volley of rich oaths, both Irish and American (some of which I had never heard before) came rolling out of the little stable. I went shame-facedly down to the shouting. Rowe's face was purple with rage and his neck was swollen up. "Just who in the hell has made a mess of this nice little mare?" (As if he didn't know.)

"Well," I gulped, "As a matter of fact, I did. I thought Mistletoe needed a little clipping."

Rowe replied, "Maybe she did need a trim, but you have shaved her! She is plain naked and that's God's own truth! I would be ashamed to appear at a hunt meet and ride a horse looking like that. In fact, I won't van her anywhere. That's final."

I pleaded with Rowe and finally persuaded him to load Mistletoe and take the mare down to the meet in the Vicmead's Middletown country. But Rowe parked half a mile away from the other vans. He sullenly unloaded Mistletoe and tightened her girth. As I mounted this hairless freak, Rowe sternly lectured me, "Now, listen to me. Don't you stand around lollygagging at the checks: keep that mare moving all the time or she'll freeze to death. Don't hang around after the hunt is over. Bring her right back to me so I can get a blanket on her, that is, if she is still alive."

I mounted without Rowe's help or his usual word of encouragement. I trotted off on down to the meet. When Bob Peoples saw me, he almost fell off his horse laughing. Indeed everybody at the meet split their sides. Poor Mistletoe stood there with her head down and her tail between her legs. Of course, there were plenty of comments.

Someone said, "Mistletoe looks like a hotdog but without the mustard."

Another foxhunter who was always immaculately turned out and rode well clipped horses said, "Bill, you should get that mare a brassiere and panties rather than letting her run around bare naked."

Another wag commented, "The last time I saw a pink horse was when I was too well served at the Columbus Inn."

Someone else added, "Look, it's Lady Godiva in reverse." Other wits aimed gibes at Mistletoe and me all afternoon. At first, I hung back because I was afraid that the Master, a well known animal lover, would send me right out of the field. Some of the older members did mutter as they distanced themselves from me, "It is a disgrace to the Vicmead to have a pink horse in our field."

But, Mistletoe, bless her heart, quickly got over her embarrassment and her nakedness. Once the actual hunting started, she went right on just as if she was not running around with nothing on. After the hunt, I brought her back to Rowe who clapped a blanket over her almost before I could slide out of the saddle.

She eventually grew her coat back. But, I never, never, from that day on, attempted to clip Mistletoe or indeed any of the other horses.

However, I did have another experience with clipping that was equally disastrous.

A friend ended up with a small Mexican burro. I think he got it to introduce riding to his two little children. Eventually the burro was foisted off on me. The animal was not much trouble, so I never got rid of her as I probably should have. She was stubborn as mules and burros are known to be. For instance, she adamantly refused to come into the warmth of my barn even on the coldest winter night, preferring to stand in the lee of the barn with the bitter wind blowing her tail toward the front of her with snow piled on her back from her long grey ears to her black tail. On the other hand, in the summertime she would stand out in the blazing sun, blinking and switching her tail but not coming into the cool of the barn or even moving into the shade of the trees.

One Saturday, I was given the job of clipping our dogs. Just as I was finishing, out of the corner of my eye, I saw Rosario, for that is what the burro was called, standing in the hot July sunshine. Her matted gray hair was about six inches long. I felt compassion for this poor sweltering beast. I ran an extension cord out to where Rosario stood and started clipping her.

At the end of half an hour, Rosario was standing in pile of six to eight inches of her grey hair. I could clearly see the cross running across her shoulders and down her back (reputed to be a holy mark that God had conferred on these lowly creatures since one of them carried Jesus on his fatal journey into Jerusalem). Be that as it may, Rosario was quite as naked as Mistletoe had been so many years before. Only, her skin was grey instead of pink. I was quite pleased with myself. What a good deed I have done, I smugly thought as I put the dog clippers and the extension cord away.

However, the flies that buzzed around Rosario soon found that she was now a deliciously unprotected morsel. They came from miles around to feed on her. The burro could only protect that part of herself that lay within the radius of her short tail. Elsewhere, she was defenseless against the flies that swarmed all over her. She rubbed herself on the fences, trees and bushes to relieve herself momentarily of the scourge of these flies. Pretty soon, the flies had broken through her tough skin. In thirty-six hours, Rosario was covered with sores, some of which became infected.

I again called Dr. Arnold. Once again he came right over. A series of oaths, similar to what I heard coming from the mouth of Rowe O'Neal, punctuated the stillness of Corner Ketch. I came on out of the house to meet a red-faced Dr. Arnold. "Just who in the hell has clipped this burro and why in God's name, if I might be so bold as to ask!"

I replied meekly, "I did, Dr. Arnold. I thought she was dying of the heat."

Dr. Arnold replied with withering sarcasm, "God made this burro. He also made some asses in this world, you among them! God gave this beast a thick coat of hair. Her natural habitat has a very hot climate. Now, what do you suppose God had in mind when He gave her a thick coat of hair? Did God do this to torment the beast by making it hot for her in the summertime? Or do you suppose that this coat of hair was given to this animal by God Almighty to insulate her both in summer and winter?"

I answered weakly, "I never thought of that."

Dr. Arnold said nothing more for the moment. He opened his black bag and proceeded to cleanse all the wounds of the poor little burro. He gave her an antihistamine to lessen her constant itching from the sores. When he had medicated her to the extent he could to remedy and relieve her pain and suffering, he turned right around to me, "Now, let me address myself to you. You are the only real jackass on this place! You will do penance for your stupidity. I am ordering you to clean a stall out in your barn. You will then keep this little burro in a clean stall until her wounds completely heal up and her coat grows out. You are to keep the barn spotlessly clean. Spray her stall for flies twice a day. You are also to cleanse and medicate all these wounds twice a day. You are to feed her on good hay and provide her with plenty of clean fresh water. I will come by every once in a while to see that my orders are being carried out to the letter. If my orders are not carried out to the letter, you can look forward to a citation for cruelty to animals. Is all that clear? Is there any part of this that you don't understand?"

I replied lamely, "I understand, Dr. Arnold." I spent the next six weeks tending to the burro who lived in cool dark comfort in a sparkling clean stall in the barn.

Years later, Rowe suddenly died of a fatal heart attack. I was devastated. He had been a true and faithful friend who had helped me immeasurably. Among other things, I had to take my big hunter, Tug, back to my barn at Corner Ketch. I also wondered how I was going to get him clipped. But I had finally learned my lesson and knew that I could not and should not clip him myself. In the meanwhile, I again had the pleasure of caring for a hunting horse myself.

I always liked feeding horses. It was fun to come out to the stable in the morning and see the horses with their big heads arched out of their stalls, stamping their feet in anticipation of their ration of grain. I liked cleaning horses by brushing them until their coats glowed, and their tails and manes were clean, and their feet, which they would readily pick up, were picked out.

Rowe had told me early on that the last thing I should do every night when I had horses on the place was to go out and make sure they were okay because when a horse lies down, it can, at times, get its legs up against the walls of the stall in such a way that it cannot get up. On one occasion I found that had actually happened. The only thing to do was to physically drag the horse around so it could get its feet back under it. Then the horse could get back up on its feet again. That averted a serious disaster.

The real pleasure in going out every night was in large part to go into the stable to hear the horses quietly munching their hay in the dark stillness of the big barn. There were never any rats or mice in my barn at Corner Ketch mostly because a 10-foot black snake lived in the rafters and kept the rodent population, as well as the pigeon population, in check. When I would turn the lights on in the hayloft, the snake would slide softly and sinuously into his hole in the corner of the stone wall of the barn, but he and I had a good relationship.

I also enjoyed cleaning tack with saddle soap. I liked having my tack room all clean with each saddle, bridle, halter, girth, and martingale hanging in its place. I liked to keep the floor of the stable and tack room cleanly swept down and a little bit damp from a dash of water. A clean stable has a wonderful smell.

There were hundreds of other things I liked about having a horse or horses on the place. I have not mentioned the pleasure of just riding cross country in the fall when the trees are all aflame, or galloping across green pastures in the spring when the trees are just about to come into leaf and everything is wonderfully fresh. In the dead of winter when there is new fallen snow on the ground, there is no foxhunting, but horses love to go out and kick up the snow. I love to walk out in the moonlight on a cold winter night and hear the high pitched barking of a fox. I like to watch a fox himself hunt and catch bugs and mice in a hedgerow or watch a litter of little fox cubs play and tussle in the sunlight near the den under the ever watchful eye of the mother fox. All of this was an escape for me out of the everyday world and into the magic world of horses and foxhunting. Still, I had not answered the problem of how to get Tug clipped.

Then, one fine Sunday morning early in September, I heard the cheery sound of a hunting horn coming from the hills on the far side of the White Clay Creek. I popped a saddle on Tug and eventually caught up with Ralph Reeber and his brothers, cousins and friends, for it was Ralph who was blowing the horn. Ralph lived in nearby Landenberg in the White Clay Creek Valley. He kept and keeps a pack of American hounds in an old barn on the far side of the White Clay. He hunted the whole White Clay Creek Valley and the country roundabout it. Ralph had it all to himself since the White Clay Creek Valley acreage had been bought up years ago by the Pennsylvania Railroad for a reservoir that had never been built. Ralph invited me that day to join his little band of foxhunters. I spent that Sunday and scores of Sundays thereafter with him and his friends hunting all through the White Clay Creek Valley. Ralph would go out at 10:00 a.m. on Sunday and not come in until 4:00 o'clock or so. His American hounds were perfect for hunting the rugged country found in the White Clay Creek Valley. There were foxes aplenty so that it was a rare day indeed when Ralph came up blank. He was and is a knowledgeable, skillful and passionate foxhunter.

One day, I had the temerity to say, "Ralph, can you clip Tug?" (I noted that his horse was sporting a fresh neat clip.)

He said, "Yep, I sure can." Thus, I would come home at night after my labors in the law office and would see a light in the barn. There would be Ralph, like Rowe, standing on a chair quietly clipping Tug who was standing still with his skin twitching slightly as Ralph's smooth running horse clippers tickled his skin.

One time, in early February, after Ralph had finished clipping, we were in the house having a beer. I asked Ralph, "Just how many times have you been out hunting this year?"

He smiled, "I've been out eighty-three times since August."

Ralph, in turn, took a pull on his beer and his cigarette and asked me, with a slight twinkle, "Bill, and just how many times have you been out?"

I had not kept a careful count but I allowed, "Certainly not more than fifteen times." We both thought about that silently for a while since Ralph was spare with words.

After Ralph had packed up his clippers and had gone on home, I thought about the situation. Just who was getting most out of life? Ralph had hunted eighty-three times and would undoubtedly hunt more than a hundred times before foxhunting ended on St. Patrick's Day. I would probably end up hunting not more than twenty times. I wondered whether I was wasting my life chasing after law cases when what I really liked to do was chase after foxes. On the other hand, Ralph, I knew, worked at Atlantic Aviation on the interiors of planes that were being outfitted or refurbished. I thought long and hard. I decided that there wasn't anything that I could do about the situation. I had come too far along the path that I had chosen to turn back. Besides, I did not have the ability to be a full time foxhunter. On the other hand, Ralph, for his part, had chosen his role in life and could not now turn back and become a lawyer. I remember what Rowe once told me: "Never, never look back once you are safely over a jump."

As I thought more about it, I decided that the only thing to do was to make the best of things by hunting whenever I could and not envy someone else's situation. That is what I have done. But, rest assured, I have not clipped any more horses or other animals except for a few dogs.

OCTORIAN MEMORIES

No hour of life is lost that is spent in the saddle.
WINSTON CHURCHILL

Over the years, I have hunted mostly with Vicmead or Cheshire. Unfortunately, I never was able to travel around to other hunts nearly as often as I would have liked. One problem was that except for holidays, I only could hunt on Saturdays. I managed to slide out of the office on a weekday on very rare occasions. Also, it was quite a job to arrange a van to transport a horse to another hunt's meeting place, get there one's self, hunt, and then come all the way home that same night. It was usually just plain easier to foxhunt with one's own hunt. In my case, that was originally the Vicmead and later the Cheshire hounds at Unionville. However, I hunted once or twice in Virginia and more than once with the Greenspring Hounds or the Elkridge Harford Hounds in Maryland. I hunted several times with Ham Fox, Master of the Wicomico Hounds, at various places down on the Eastern Shore and lower Delaware. I also hunted fairly often with Ralph Reeber, his brothers, and friends in the White Clay Creek Valley on Sundays.

The origins of this account of a fine day of hunting started when my law partner, Richard I.G. Jones, told me earlier in the week that he, his wife, Annie, my goddaughter, Braxton, and their son, Brett, were all going to make a day of it with the Andrew's Bridge Hunt on Saturday in the Octorara Country north of Unionville. He suggested that I take up Robert Crompton's, the MFH, longstanding invitation to come up once again to hunt with his Andrew's Bridge Hounds.

Then, on Friday, I got a call from Stephanie Carpenter. "Bill, my 14-year Lucinda is, as you know, a good young rider. She's been asked by Braxton, her best friend, to try foxhunting. In fact, Lucinda has a new small horse, Gatsby. She would like to hunt Saturday with the Jones family at Andrew's Bridge. Could you squeeze Gatsby in your trailer?"

Tug. Photographer: Unknown.

I replied, "Of course, Steph. I'm always delighted when a youngster wants to try foxhunting. I only wish I could get my daughter, Annie, to try it."

Steph replied, "Thanks, Bill. As for Annie, just wait. Her time for foxhunting with you will come. You'll see."

Because my hunter, Tug, stood 18 hands high and took up both stalls of my trailer, I knew I would have to make two trips. But I assured Stephanie, "Tell Lucinda to have Gatsby ready at 8:00 a.m. I will be there."

Thus, on Saturday morning, my alarm went off at 7:00 a.m. After a cup of coffee, I was off in my International pickup to get my horse trailer. As I drove over to get the trailer, I wondered how Lucinda's horse got the name of Scott Fitzgerald's tragic hero. At 8:00 a.m., I got to Carpenter's. Gatsby, a good looking and sensible horse, and Lucinda were ready and waiting. I said to Lucinda, "Hi. Ready for the greatest day of your life?"

She replied, "Sure am!" We loaded her horse without difficulty. She and Gatsby were going to spend the weekend with Braxton, so Lucinda had an overnight bag for herself and a blanket for Gatsby.

Just before we left, I privately promised Stephanie, a typical "worried mom," "I'll telephone you right after the hunt if Lucinda does not do so. She'll be fine and do great, don't you worry." Lucinda and I then were off to the Jones' house in Unionville, arriving there at 8:30 a.m. Gatsby was unloaded and put in a spare stall until 10:00 a.m. or so when he would go in Richie's large gooseneck trailer with the Jones' horses. In the meanwhile, I had a stout

William Prickett on Tug.
Photographer: Unknown.

breakfast cooked by the Jones' cook, Izzie, of ham, eggs, toast, and juice with those of the Jones family who were going hunting—Richie, Annie, Brett, Braxton, and of course, Lucinda.

I then piled back in my truck and started on back to the Vicmead Hunt Club Stable to pick up Tug. My truck was losing power and "pinging" terribly. I also saw to my horror that the heat indicator had gone way up the red line, so I pulled into the gas station at Unionville.

"Your fan belt is broken," the smiling attendant said. "No big deal. You'll make hunting today. I just wish I was able to get to go out." Thus, my picking up Lucinda and her pony, while ostensibly an act of hunting kindness, had carried its own reward. If I had not had to come back to the Vicmead in Greenville after delivering Gatsby, I might well have been in the wilds of the Octorara Country with an overheated truck and an over anxious horse. As it was, in a trice, the garage had me fixed up with a new fan belt. "Good hunting," the attendant called out as I drove away. Thus, I went "coolly" back to the Vicmead and picked up Tug. He was waiting—standing in his stall fully tacked, stamping his big feet and trembling with anticipation and impatience since he knew he would be hunting this day.

I had prudently gotten written directions and a map from Richie to locate the Bell Bank meet. I drove down Route 1 to Route 896, made a right on Route 896, and drove to Russellville. Beyond that, I made a left and then a right. As I came cautiously down a long steep hill toward a one-lane bridge over the Octorara, I could see a gaggle of vans and trailers drawn up in a field across the valley. I

William Prickett on Tug.
Photographer: Unknown.

drove over, pulled in, and parked.

Tug, snorting and stomping, backed his way off the trailer. After tightening the girth, I went to a high bank to mount up. Once aboard, I rode over to say hello to my hunting host, Bob Crompton, MFH, who said, "Bill, you are most welcome. I only hope we can show you some real sport today. I understand you and Richie are introducing Ruly and Steph Carpenter's daughter to foxhunting today. Let's hope she gets hooked. When are you going to get your Annie to come out?" Bob Crompton was dressed in the Lincoln green coat which is worn by the Andrew's Bridge Hunt (rather than a pink coat), perhaps a deference to the Amish farmers whose permission to hunt over their well kept fields is necessary. Bob was on his horse in the midst of the pack of gingerbread colored Penn Marydel hounds. A whip, Mike Quinlan, kept a benign eye on the pack, occasionally flicking his whip over the head of a straying hound, sending him back to the master and the pack. There were a dozen foxhunting acquaintances from years ago but there was no time to say hello at that point. Just as Bob blew his horn, Richie bumped on in with his gooseneck loaded to the gills. Annie and Richie had found that they had an additional serviceable hunter, so they had called Dolly Fisher, whose hunter had gone lame, and offered her this mount. Thus, Dolly came with her daughter, Katherine, home from boarding school. Quickly, all the Jones' horses were unloaded, saddled up, and mounted. Just then, Richie's brother, Russell Jones, and his son, Michael, arrived. When they too were mounted, we all galloped up the large hill to the place where the hunt was just about to get underway.

When I had gotten up that morning, the sky was somewhat overcast. There were predictions of rain. However, these dour indications had vanished. It was a beautiful day without the blustery wind so characteristic of March. The temperature hovered in the low 40's. The heavy rains of the week before had completely eradicated the winter snows, so footing would be good. It looked like it would be a good day for foxhunting. However, as we started, someone dolefully remarked, "I doubt that this will be a good hunting day. In fact, there probably won't be any scent at all." I, for one, had long since disregarded prognostications about scent, be they good or bad. At least in my view, the only safe way to determine whether scent is good, bad, indifferent, or glorious is simply to come out and see for one's self.

A rider who shared my outlook said, "Well, it's always good to be out, right Counselor?"

"You betcha," I replied.

We were soon hunting through fields surrounded by stout fences. Memories came back to me from previous occasions when I hunted up in the Octorara Country. The hounds indicated that a fox had been by sometime before. The mixed dog and bitch pack hunted with determination and with little direction from Bob and his whips. The field of about twenty trotted along well behind Bob so as not to interfere with his hunting concentration. I checked on my charge, Lucinda. No need to do so: she was chatting happily with her long time buddies, Braxton and Katherine.

Eventually, we crossed one of the wheel-smooth slippery tar roads and turned right. Bob then cast his hounds. Suddenly, from the bottom of a small depression covered with second growth and honeysuckle, came unmistakable sounds that made it clear the hounds had struck a good line. They were off and running. As we came galloping toward the road, we came across a single strand of barbed wire lying on the ground. It got tangled on Annie Jones' horse's right foot. I jumped down and tried to help untangle the wire from the frightened horse's foot. I was just pulling out my wire cutters when a more experienced horseman came along, jumped down, and with one dexterous twist, successfully pulled the wire free. Annie's horse mercifully was not hurt.

In the meanwhile, the hounds were making a valiant noise in the bottom. I quickly found a high bank and remounted. Quite suddenly, a beautiful white tipped honey-colored fox burst right into our view, running swiftly south and west. However, the fox quickly turned right. Bob called the hounds to him by calls on his horn and put them on the line. Then the fox was viewed again running north and slightly eastward across the road. The hounds set off at a terrific pace. We were not far behind. We also crossed the road and galloped after Bob, the whips and the hounds in a generally northeast direction. After we had gone a couple of miles, the field became scattered. I saw Lucinda cantering along with Katherine and Braxton. It had become a run in which one could go in the direction and at the pace that suited one best.

It is impossible to describe all the things that happened on that glorious two-hour run. All I can do is remember some vignettes: a big fence which Annie Jones led everyone over; Dolly Fisher helping adjust the saddle on Brett's shaggy pony which had slid backward; Lucinda's gallant little horse, Gatsby, standing well back from a three-railer, tucking nimbly and then turning adroitly to the right two strides after the jump; a group huddled around Michael Jones whose pony had swerved on the ever slippery tar road and had come down—pony, saddle, and small boy and all; Michael's father, Russell, and his Uncle Richie were there in their Lincoln green hunting coats clustered around the fallen eight-year old. They both motioned all of us to go on; a two-mile long gallop up a woods path entirely by myself, wondering whether I had lost the hounds, the Master, and the field for the balance of the afternoon; then coming out at the far end and finding that Bob and others more knowledgeable about the country had taken a shortcut and were there well before me.

There were eight or ten hunters who had followed closely behind Bob. The hounds could be heard still driving hard but were way, way out ahead of us and far to the right. Bob and the whips set out at a gallop to get with the hounds. The rest of the field was strung out behind going in all different directions. Finally, we caught sight of the hounds running in a field far over to our right. The hounds were coming our way: clearly the fox had made his turn and was coming back. We galloped on down a steep hill, splashed across a stream, and then up the other side, and then through alternately brown plowed fields and bright green fields. The hounds were still hunting under Bob's guidance, but they no longer had a fresh line. By this time, even the stoutest horses, including Tug, were breathing hard. Riders were damp with sweat. Our coats were soaked through. Though my horse was still eager and full of spunk, he had had a long exhilarating run punctuated with plenty of jumps.

Bob summoned his hounds and cast the pack into a brambly bottom. They began

hunting again, but this time, at a more leisurely pace. Someone said that this certainly was a "two-horse" day. Eventually, we came up on the main road and caught up with most of the rest of the field, though some had had quite enough and had already turned homeward. We found out that Michael was only a little shaken up by his long slide along the tar road (and by having his pony go partially over him).

Some previous year, on a similar exhilarating run, I had lost my Timex watch in this very area. I kept my eyes peeled for it and asked others to be on the lookout for my lost chronometer. Everyone had stories to recount since it had been an old-fashioned point-to-point with everybody taking their own line. All the young entries, Lucinda, Braxton, and Katherine, had all accounted well for themselves.

Bob was carefully hunting his hounds on what was now an old line. We went slowly back over the country that we had just come up so rapidly. Finally, we came back virtually to the spot where we had originally started and found that our fox had gone to earth. Bob dismounted and blew "Gone to Earth" on his horn over the fox's hole. He walked back to his horse, calling and praising each of his hounds before jumping back on his horse.

Bob then asked the field, "Well, what about it? Shall we scare up another fox? The day is still young." But, it was agreed all the way around that we had already had a full and glorious day. If by chance we struck another fox such as the one that we had followed for almost three hours at such a brisk pace, we might founder our horses (and indeed, hunters such as myself). Bob, there-

William Prickett on Tug at Vicmead Kennels, Middletown, Delaware. Photographer: Unknown.

fore, assembled his hounds and put them in the hound truck which had been brought up. We ambled backward down the sides of the treacherous tar road, savoring the quiet pleasure of the end of a good day of foxhunting. Around us stretched the late winter countryside of the Octorara Country. On the horizon, a bearded Amish man dressed all in black stood out against the large white clouds, plowing his fields and turning over the rich brown earth with a team of four draft horses.

There was a hint of impending spring, though even in the deepest bottoms the green skunk cabbage had not yet begun to peep out. The temperature had turned colder as we rode back the last couple of miles retracing our steps that we had covered at such a rapid pace a couple of hours ago. When we got to the vans, everyone dismounted a trifle wearily. After blankets, coolers, or sheets were thrown over the tired horses, the horses and ponies were loaded into vans and trailers. I walked over to Bob. "Thanks Robert for another day of wonderful hunting. I will mail you the capping fee. I knew that the capping fee was a drop in the bucket; but hounds must eat, and horses must be fed, as old Mrs. Bedford at Elkridge-Harford Hunt used to say as she gathered up a $25 capping fee from visiting foxhunters."

Bob said "Thanks for coming out with us. It was a pretty good day, wasn't it? No need to send the cap."

Richie, as he was driving his gooseneck trailer away, suddenly pulled up, stopped, got out, and trotted back over to me. He handed me a ham and cheese sandwich, "It's an extra sandwich. Enjoy." I munched the sandwich with great pleasure as I drove slowly back southward through the Octorara Country and rejoined Route 1 for the trip back to the Vicmead. There, I immediately telephoned Stephanie, "Steph, Lucinda is fine. She did not fall, and she and Gatsby had a wonderful day of foxhunting together."

Stephanie replied, "Thanks for the call. I was sure Lucinda would do well, but part of a mom's job is to worry."

I said, "I only wished that I could have persuaded Annie to come with me."

Stephanie said, "Well, maybe some day she will."

PART THREE

THE CHESHIRE YEARS
1976-1998

THE CHESHIRE YEARS
1976-1998

Mr. Stewart's Cheshire Hounds (often simply referred to as Unionville) was founded in 1912 by Mrs. John B. Hannum's stepfather, Mr. Plunkett Stewart. Cheshire's hunting country basically lies north and west of Unionville in the turf-covered rolling hills of Chester County, Pennsylvania, roughly bordered by Route 1 to the south, Route 41 to the west, Route 10 to the north, and Route 52 to the east. The country consists of pastures, and hay and corn fields which are interspersed with large forested areas and woods. It is splendid country for all sorts of horse activity, including, of course, foxhunting.

When Vicmead began to falter, my law partner, Richard Jones, a horseman and a most knowledgeable and long time foxhunter with Cheshire, urged me to come to Unionville. I was diffident, not only because of my modest riding ability but also because of Cheshire's big stiff fences. In addition the Cheshire field consisted expert horsemen and women, most of whom rode every day and had ridden and foxhunted all their lives. Many were timber, show or 3-day event riders or polo players. Still, the Jones and Hannum families and many others, thank goodness, prevailed on me to come and try hunting with Cheshire.

I found to my surprise a genuine welcome, not only from the Cheshire field, but Mrs. Hannum herself and the hunting staff. Equally important, Bruce Miller, a frequent Cheshire Field Master, stabled my horse and gave me constant encouragement. Later, Nancy Miller took on the job of caring for my horse and continues today giving me necessary support. Thus, I have been fortunate enough to hunt with Cheshire, one of the most prominent hunts in America for the balance of my hunting career, as these accounts will show.

Tis not too late to seek a newer world.

TENNYSON, ULYSSES

VINCE DUGAN

If he a foxhunter, I likes him.
JORROCKS

I had heard a lot about colorful Vince Dugan long before I actually had occasion to meet him. Vince, an Irish-American horseman of about my own age, is a very successful horse dealer with a large stable on Street Road in the Unionville country.

For years, I had had no need of Vince's services. However, long after Fanny had been returned to her rightful owner and Tug, her colt, had had to be put down after years of hunting, I was hard pressed to find a hunting horse. Sadly, I no longer had Rowe O'Neal to help me find one. Even though I had stabled Tug with Nancy Miller, I had not yet come to depend on her as I later would. But, I asked her to keep an eye out for a good hunting horse. Nancy said, "I will but it's going to take time to find a horse that you can hunt successfully." I had a far better opinion of myself as a rider than I had any right to. This account plainly proves it. I tried half a dozen horses, with no success. It was well into the hunting season and I was still without a horse of any kind.

One day when I was at the meet, Mrs. Hannum said, "Bill, are you still without a horse to hunt? Have you tried Vince Dugan? He has supplied a good number of the Cheshire field with hunting horses. See if he doesn't have something you can hunt."

I called Vince and explained my horseless state. He said, "You know, I heard 'round about of your situation," and added, "but I do not have anything at the moment except for a horse called Flash. But, Flash may not be the right horse for a rider like yourself."

Stung, I replied, "I have quite a lot of experience. Why don't I just try Flash, or whatever his name is?"

Vince replied doubtfully, "Okay, you're the boss. Come to the Cheshire Hunt meet and try Flash tomorrow."

Vincent Dugan. Photographer: Unknown.

The next day, at the Cheshire Hunt meet, Vince led Flash out of the van: Flash was flashy indeed. He sort of rolled his eyes and snorted as he pranced about. As Vince put one of his saddles on the gelding, he cautioned me, "Now, Billy Boy, this here horse will jump anything and everything that you may come across in the Unionville country. But, Flash doesn't take to standing around at a check. All you have to do . . . just keep old Flash moving. Don't try to make him stand: he just don't take to it, don't you see? Keep him walking about and you'll both be okay, just you wait and see, my fine laddie. Good hunting. By the way, I myself am coming out today. I just might keep an eye on you and Flash to see how you two get on together. Are you sure you are up to Flash? He's quite a handful."

I replied somewhat haughtily, "Of course. I can handle Flash. Just you wait and see."

I somehow managed to get aboard Flash with the help of Vince and a couple of his stable girls. I went right over to say my good mornings to Mrs. Hannum, the staff, and some of my hunting friends. They were pleased to see me out hunting again. One said, "That is a showy new steed you're on." But, mindful of Vince's admonitions, I did not reply but kept Flash right on walking, since Flash would plunge and rear if he wasn't kept moving.

We eventually moved off in response to Gerald's, the Huntsman, call on his horn. Flash, while fidgety, clearly knew something about jumping. Indeed, when we came to the first fence, I found he was all that Vince had promised, and more, a lot more. Flash would gather himself and take a hold of the bit, roar into the jump like an express train and sail on over. But Flash was hard to pull up on the other side of a fence. Vince came up at one point and said smoothly, "Are you doing okay, Sir? Flash needs an experienced rider."

I said, "Vince, I will be okay once Flash settles down." Nancy Miller passed me at one point and looked very gloomily at me and at Flash who was prancing about.

Things went sort of all right for about an hour. Of course, we had not yet come across a fox. We then came to a narrow path in the woods that led down a rather steep hill. Alongside this hill, there was a pond. At the far end of the path, there was a small panel that had to be jumped. Everybody had to stop and wait their turn to jump this fence. Right then I knew that I was in deep trouble because Flash was already making it quite clear that Vince had been dead right. This horse did not like standing still at a check one little bit. First, he backed up and bumped smartly into a well mannered horse that was standing quietly behind us. Then Flash went brusquely forward and tried to push around another horse standing right in front of us, but the path was too narrow. Then Flash began to circle rapidly around and around. One of his back feet slid off the path. I managed to pull on the reins and get him back up on the path. Then he began to snort and rear. I pulled him up sharply, shouting calming words like "Whoa, Sir, Whoa, you brute!" Flash responded by again backing up. In fact, he backed right dab off the path.

By now, all eyes were on us. The hill was so steep that Flash tumbled over sideways. In an instant both of us were cartwheeling head over heels down toward the pond. I somehow managed to extricate my feet from the stirrups and continued my free fall on down the hill toward the pond, but without Flash. My downward descent was stopped by a sturdy poplar tree. Flash somehow had also managed to stop his tumbling course toward the pond and began to scramble back up the hill. I could see my fellow foxhunters peering in horror over the edge of the path at what must have appeared to be a fatal disaster for both horse and rider. Someone managed to reach out and catch Flash's bridle as he lunged back up and over the lip of the path. I clambered slowly up, hand over hand. A couple of hands reached out and pulled me back up and over onto the path. Vince had come back to the scene of the disaster. Vince loudly asked, "How did Flash come back up over the edge? Was the rider pulling back on the reins? It's a mercy that neither Flash nor the gentleman was hurt!"

Then Vince turned to me and said, "If you be all right, Sir, why don't you mount my horse? I'll ride Flash!"

We switched horses. Unfortunately, Vince, a wonderful rider, had ridden out that day on a young green horse just to try him with hounds. Thus, when the green horse and I came to the low jump that had been the starting point of all my troubles, Vince's horse gave a mighty jump. The jump left me totally behind and off I tumbled!

My wind was knocked out of me. As I lay wiggling, gasping like a fish out of water, a veterinarian, slid out of her saddle and came over and knelt beside me. "Are you hurt? If so, where?"

I opened one eye and saw who it was. "Yes, Doc," I replied, "I am injured."

She said, "What is it and where?" I answered, "I have chronic athlete's foot. It's on my left foot, or maybe it's the right. Take a peek, would you, Doc?"

The veterinarian turned around and said to one and all, "Does anybody have a pair of wire cutters? I have a good mind to roll this joker over and cure his sense of humor with one snip!"

Well, I was picked up and stuck back on the young green horse, but I had had quite enough of trying to ride Vince's horses at least for that day. I did manage to get back to Vince's stable without any more adventures. As I was untacking Vince's horse, I could hear Vince talking to his giggling stable girls in the tack room, "Well, this here Mr. Prickett just ain't the rider he thinks he is. Flash was too much horse for him. Mr. Prickett did just what I told him not to do—that is, he left Flash standing in a line of horses. He begins to fret so Mr. Prickett here begins to pull back on the reins, standing in his stirrups, shouting, 'Whoa, Goddamit, whoa!' So, of course, sure as horse shoes, Flash backs up and dumps hisself right off the path, and they roll down the hill, almost plunk into the drink. It's a mercy that Mr. Prickett didn't kill himself and Flash and break my good saddle right into the bargain! What a man has to put up with these days in the horse business. I have a mind to become a mailman, a politico, or a priest!"

I cleared my throat and came on into the tack room.

Vince turned around and said solicitously, "Well, now, Sir, all's well that ends well, I always say. Seriously, I don't think that Flash will suit you at all. But I have a horse coming in later this month that might just be okay for you."

Thus, I was still without a hunting horse. Then, quite out of the blue about three weeks later, a friend, one of the best riders in the Cheshire field, called me. "Bill, Vince

William Prickett, Babar, Nancy Miller, Fred and Mail Dog. Photographer: Caroline Prickett, Chesapeake City, Maryland.

Prevouis page: *Nancy Miller, acting Field Master on Liberty.* Photographer: James Graham, Montchanin, Delaware.

Dugan has a large German warm blood that just might suit you. You should give Vince a call and see if maybe the horse would suit."

Warily, I called Vince. Vince already knew what I was calling about, "Yes, indeed. I think I may have a horse you could manage. Tell you what, why don't you meet me tomorrow at the meet?"

The next day, I drove on out to where the Cheshire Hounds was meeting. Vince's van was there. When the door opened, the biggest horse I had ever seen backed ponderously out of Vince's van. The horse seemed quiet enough as my saddle was put up and on and an extra large girth was cinched up.

I asked Vince, "Has this horse ever hunted before?"

He replied genially, "Oh, yes, my, yes, I believe so. He's hunted with all packs round about here. He's known to everyone and a great favorite he is in all the fields."

"By the way, Vince, what's the name of this giant?"

He replied, "Would you believe it? I don't rightly remember right now, but it's something German, like Oscar or Fritz. Anyways, have a good hunt whatever this horse's name is!"

Just then the horn sounded. It was time to mount up. I climbed up on the roof of my car and slid down on the horse and into the saddle while Vince held him steady. The ground was a long, long way down. I trotted over to the group of Cheshire foxhunters. Everyone looked up at my giant mount with awe. Pretty soon we set out. Oscar or Fritz seemed willing enough, but not very knowledgeable about hunting. He jumped several fences, without any difficulty. Indeed, being 18-hands high meant that he could pretty much step over anything but a 3-railer.

However, when we came to a small stream in a woods, he pricked his ears up. When we got to the very edge of this tiny trickle, Oscar suddenly put on his brakes with full force and stopped dead. I had some inkling as we got close to this little brook that he was going to do something like that so that I was ready and did not come off, though I slid up on his big neck almost to his ears. I then turned him around and urged him to go over this streamlet. Again he stopped and adamantly refused not only to jump it but to step across. He refused even when a couple of friends, who were keeping a friendly eye on me since I was out for the first time on this huge steed, gave me a lead. He still refused. Then, another friend took her crop and gave him a sound whack on his ample rump, saying "Go on now, Bismark, or whatever your name is!" But, he never did go over that small stream. Finally, I just had to go around another way.

I hunted him successfully all that day but this cyclopean horse adamantly refused to cross all the other little streams, brooks and even puddles.

Back at the van, Vince called to me as I threw the reins down to him, loosened the girth, pulled up the stirrups and jumped down all the way to the ground, "Now, Sir, how did Oscar or Rudolph go for you?"

I said, "Well enough, indeed, Vince, except that he totally refused to cross a tiny stream. I even got a couple of people to give me a lead and we gave him a sound whack with a crop, but he still wouldn't go across. As a matter of fact, I couldn't get him to cross any stream or brook or even walk through a puddle. You told me he had hunted all before. Where was it, in a desert?"

He replied evenly, "Well, Sir, when this here horse was hunted, it was a dry season, don't you know?"

It turned out that Peter the Great (for that is what I called him) had been raised and trained as an open jumper.

Nancy Miller tried Peter the Great and approved. He vetted sound. So, I bought Peter. He was easy to ride and loved to hunt. He quickly learned to jump or cross streams though I always detected a momentary hesitation as we came to a stream. He and I had five wonderful seasons together since, for all his size, he was handy and agile. Unfortunately, I got a call early one morning from Nancy Miller, who told me that Peter the Great died in the field the previous night where he was turned out. He had a twisted gut. It is an odd, often fatal condition that horses occasionally get totally spontaneously.

But my dealings with Vince were not yet over. My daughter, Annie, had been riding ever since she was six or so. My entreaties that she come out foxhunting with me fell on deaf ears. Annie adamantly refused. "Dad, foxhunting is not cool." Eventually there came a time when she was thirteen, and she needed a show horse instead of Grey, her fat pony.

Vince said when I telephoned him, "Why, Sir. I just happen to have a fine mare, Oz, that will suit little Miss Annie to a T. Mark my words!"

I said to Vince, "But, will this Oz hunt? I really want Annie to try hunting."

Vince replied, "My, yes. This horse will do it all. Showing, foxhunting, dressage, you name it. This horse will make a foxhunter out of your Annie if that be your wish." However, when I had Oz vetted, the vet would not pass her.

When I reported this to Vince, he said testily, "May the Good Lord forgive that dumb horse doctor. That vet wouldn't pass her own grandmother. But, I'll tell you what I'm going to do for you and your Annie. I'll lease Oz to you by the month. If she ever takes one lame step or just doesn't suit, you just turn Oz back to old Vince. Now, ain't that a handsome proposition!"

Indeed, that was an entirely satisfactory proposition so far as I was concerned. (Of course, Annie had a hankering to own her own horse outright as opposed to just leasing a horse.) After eighteen months, Oz did go lame. I returned Oz to Vince. Vince did not repine: he had gotten 18 months of lease payments out of me for a horse that no vet would pass. I heard later that Vince had gotten Oz sound again and leased her out again (and again).

When she was 15, Annie began to look for a serious show horse. There came a Tuesday when, quite out of the blue, I got a call at the office. After chatting me up, Annie said quite casually, "Oh, Dad, by the way, could you meet me at Vince Dugan's this afternoon at 3:30 p.m. sharp?"

I replied, "Sure, Annie." (After all, what are fathers for?) I suspected that Annie had run into a horse that she had to have. I managed to rearrange my somewhat full schedule and drove on out to Vince's large stable.

When I came into the stable, there was Annie with her arms around the neck of a big horse. Vince was standing nearby, with a piece of straw in his teeth, looking sideways at this show of affection, with just a tinge of smile. I saw right away that I was going to have a hard time bargaining with Vince who was already armed with a formidable bar-

Mr. Stewart's Cheshire Foxhounds

will meet

OCTOBER, 1995

Tuesday, 3rd	Runnymede	8:00 AM
Thursday, 5th	Mr. David Davis' Gate (Fairview School House)	8:00 AM
Saturday, 7th	The Kennels-Chester County Day	9:00 AM
	The Kennels will be open for inspection 8:00 - 10:00 AM	
Monday, 9th	(Columbus Day) Hamilton Farm on Rte. 841	8:00 AM
Tuesday, 10th	No Hunting	
Thursday, 12th	Mr. Edgar Scott	8:00 AM
Saturday, 14th	Mr. Robert E. Strawbridge (Chatham)	8:00 AM
Sunday, 15th	The Willowdale Gold Cup, Routes 926 and 82	
	Kristen Golden 444-1582. Gates open at 11:00 AM	
Monday, 16th	Pennsylvania National Horse Show - Harrisburg	
	50th Anniversary	6:00 PM
Tuesday, 17th	Mrs. March Walsh	8:00 PM
Thursday, 19th	Mr. Richard I. G. Jones	8:00 AM
Saturday, 21st	The Kennels-For benefit of Adult Night School	8:00 AM
Sunday, 22nd	Cheshire Pony Club Paper Chase at Mr. Morrow's field, Rte. 82 & Green Valley Road, 347-1809	
Tuesday, 24th	Springdell	8:00 AM
Thursday, 26th	Mr. Jefferis Gate (Hilltop View Road)	8:00 AM
Saturday, 28th	No Hunting-Opening Day of small game season	
Sunday, 29th	PHA Paper Chase at Halfway House. For information call Kathy King 444-5340	12:00 PM
Tuesday, 31st	Mr. Sam Slater	8:00 AM

Please note: Due to the extreme drought be conscious of not smoking at all during hunting or be sure every cigarette is squashed before being discarded. Please close gates, respect planted fields, and report any broken fences or damages to the Field Master. Please stay with the Field Master or stop and wait for the field to pass. Messages regarding hunting are at 347-2209.

Mrs. John B. Hannum, M.F.H.
347-2209 or 347-2186

gaining chip: he knew that my life would be downright miserable unless I bought this horse for Annie. This thoroughbred, named Sparky (True Sparkle), was a show horse. Annie wanted him more than anything in the world as only a 15-year old horse-crazy girl can.

Vince's opening offer was twice more than I had ever paid for a good hunting horse. I said, "Your price is so outrageous that we are not even going to make a counteroffer unless the horse is passed by our veterinarian."

"Suit yourself," he replied, "but don't you come blamin' good old Vince if that other show rider's father from Virginia who was lookin' at Sparky mighty sharp just yesterday calls up and takes him! Then where will ye be, Mr. Daddeo? Tell me that, won't ye now?"

I answered, "That just may happen. We'll just have to take that chance, won't we, Annie?" Annie was plainly in agony. I then said, "But tell me, Vince, can this Top Sparkle foxhunt? Answer me that."

Annie blurted out almost in tears, "Who cares about dumb old foxhunting!"

Vince said, "I think Sparky could, but I don't think you have quite sold Miss Annie on foxhunting yet!"

This time, the horse vetted sound. I said, "Annie, you have to learn how to bargain for a horse since I will not always be around, but the Vince Dugans of the world will always be there.

Mr. Stewart's Cheshire Foxhounds

will meet

OCTOBER, 1996

Tuesday, 1st	Runnymede	8:00 AM
Thursday, 3rd	Mr. Richard I. G. Jones (Doe Run)	8:00 AM
Saturday, 5th	Mr. Michael Ledyard	8:00 AM
	(Wilson Road off of Route 842)	
Tuesday, 8th	Springdell	8:00 AM
Thursday, 10th	Mr. Edgar Scott	8:00 AM
Saturday, 12th	Mr. Robert E. Strawbridge (Chatham)	8:00 AM
Sunday, 13th	Cheshire Pony Club Paper Chase—Route 82	Noon
	and Newark Road—Anne Dome 444-9675	
Monday, 14th	Columbus Day Holiday—	8:00 AM
	Mr. George Strawbridge	
Tuesday, 15th	No Hunting	————
Thursday, 17th	Mr. David Davis' Gate	8:00 AM
	(Fairview Shool House)	
Saturday, 19th	The Kennels	8:00 AM
Sunday, 20th	The Willowdale Gold Cup, Routes 926 and 82.	
	Kristen Mancuso. Gates open at 11:00 AM	
Tuesday, 22nd	Snow Hill (Mr. Gregory Bentley's—	8:00 AM
	Buck Run)	
Thursday, 24th	Dr. Elinor Jenny	8:00 AM
Saturday, 26th	No Hunting—Opening Small Game Season	————
Sunday, 27th	PHA Paper Chase—Runnymede—	Noon
	Kathy King 444-5350	
Tuesday, 29th	Irwin's Gate	8:00 AM
Thursday, 31st	Mr. Stuart Malone	8:00 AM
	(former Buck & Doe Office)	

Please note: Be conscious of not smoking at all during hunting or be sure every cigarette is squashed before being discarded. Please close gates, respect planted fields, and report any broken fences to the Field Master. Please stay with the Field Master or stop and wait for the field to pass. Messages regarding hunting are at 347-2209.

Mrs. John B. Hannum, M.F.H.
347-2209 or 347-2186

First, I suggest that we buy the horse jointly. I will loan you half the price and you can pay for your half of the horse by Christmas and birthday gifts."

Annie immediately said, "Well, when can we begin bargaining with Vince? After all, we want to get Sparky's price down, but I would die if anyone else bought Sparky!"

I explained, "Annie, your open demonstration of affection for Sparky is going to make it tough to get Vince's price down by any substantial amount. The only way to do it is to tell Vince we are looking at other horses but that we might be back to look at this particular horse. But Annie, remember, Vince is probably too smart by half to be taken in by such a feeble story. After all, he and his father before him and probably his father's father have all been horse dealers.

Annie said grimly, "Dad, I just know Vince is going to sell Sparky to someone else."

I tried to reassure her, saying, "Annie, Vince can't sell Sparky to anyone for near the price he's put on her. In any case, there are lots of other horses about."

Annie said disconsolately, "Oh, yeah. Fat lot you know, Dad!"

I was reading Churchill's autobiography at that time. I made up my mind to buy Sparky, no matter what Dugan's price, based partly on what Churchill said in a letter:

Don't give your son money. As far as you can afford it, give him horses. No one ever came to grief—except honorable grief—through riding horses. No hour of life is lost that is spent in the saddle. Young men have often been ruined through owning horses, or through backing horses, but never through riding them; unless of course they break their necks, which taken at a gallop, is a very good death to die.

Of course, I did not show Annie or Vince the Churchill quotation. After three weeks had gone by, I called Vince and, after chatting him up (which didn't deceive Vince one bit), I casually said, "Vince, by any chance do you still have a horse called Sparky?"

Vince said, "Indeed I do but, mind you, there are lots of other people been looking over Sparky. You had better come and get him right away if you really want him." (All

Mr. Stewart's Cheshire Foxhounds

will meet

FEBRUARY, 1997

Saturday, 1st	The Kennels	11:00 AM
Tuesday, 4th	Dr. Donald Wilson (north of Lemhenny's)	11:00 AM
Thursday, 6th	Dr. Christopher Lyons, Frog Hollow Road	11:00 AM
Saturday, 8th	Mr. Michael Ledyard (Park on Wilson Road)	11:00 AM
Tuesday, 11th	Springdell	11:00 AM
Thursday, 13th	Mr. Edgar Scott	11:00 AM
Saturday, 15th	Walker's Polo Field (Park in Mrs. Judy Donaldson's field on Byrd Road)	11:00 AM
Monday, 17th	President's Day Holiday—Runnymede	11:00 AM
Tuesday, 18th	No Hunting	—
Thursday, 20th	Mr. David Davis' Gate	11:00 AM
Saturday, 22nd	Mrs. Choate's Percy Pierce Barn	11:00 AM
Tuesday, 25th	Mr. Greg Bentley's Snow Hill Farm (Buck Run)	11:00 AM
Thursday, 27th	Mr. Richard I.G. Jones—Doe Run	11:00 AM

NOTE: Do NOT drive vans or trailers thru the Covered Bridge on Frog Hollow Road or over the iron bridge on duPont Road. If you do not wish to stay up with the Field Master galloping thru a cover, wait to let the field go past you then proceed at your own pace. It is frustrating to those who want to get quickly thru a crowded area to be held up by those who are "ambling". Messages regarding hunting are at 347-2209.

Mrs. John B. Hannum, M.F.H.
347-2209 or 347-2186

Annie Prickett on "Oz" at Devon Horse Show. Photographer: Kim Ketcham, Hinesburg, Vermont.

of which I, for my part, did not believe.) I reported all this to Annie who spent another sleepless night, fearing that "her" horse, Sparky, would be sold right out from under her.

Annie said, "Dad, I sure want Sparky, but I don't want to spend anything more than is necessary to get him."

I said, "Good Annie. What we will do now is to try the old 'drop check' routine on Mr. Dugan."

"What's that?" Annie asked dubiously.

"Well," I said, "we will make out a check for two-thirds of what Vince has been asking and drop it off. If the amount we offer is reasonable, Vince'll accept the check even though he knows that he is dealing with a little girl who wants Sparky terribly and a father who does not want to disappoint his little girl."

Our plan worked well; the check was promptly cashed. At that point, Annie, who is a fast learner and had learned all about the drop check technique, asked me at the closing, "Dad, did we leave any money on the table?"

I replied, "Ask Vince."

Vince, winked privately to me and said to Annie, "Nope, Annie. Not even a scotch nickel!"

Annie was very pleased with herself. She even said, "Dad, I am sorry about what I said about foxhunting. I know how much you like it. I would even consider taking Sparky out hunting, except he's too valuable a horse to risk in the hunting field chasing foxes. You don't get any blue ribbons for killing foxes. You do understand, don't you Dad?"

"Yes, Annie. I understand, but you don't quite understand about foxhunting."

Sparky worked out very well indeed for Annie. She was regularly "in the ribbons." Then, when it came time to move up to an even better horse, Annie herself patiently marketed Sparky, not back to Vince but all over the Eastern seacoast. She finally managed to get a price that was three times what "she" had paid for Sparky. In the meanwhile, Annie, now 16, had gone out and found herself an Irish open jumper, Charlie. She had successfully negotiated a price way below the original asking price and then had used the drop check method to close her deal.

Vince had watched Annie not only as a gradually improving high jumper, but as a potential horse dealer. The ultimate tribute came when Vince said, "You know, Annie, you might think of becoming a horse dealer." I had the temerity to ask Annie, "Well, Annie, some time I hope you will finally try foxhunting. You will love it, I promise you."

Annie replied, "Still plugging foxhunting? We'll see."

About three years later, my horse, Babar, went dead lame again in his right foot. No amount of vetting or special shoeing seemed to work this time. Nancy Miller, fond of Babar but anxious to see that I had a suitable foxhunting horse, said Babar's problem might be navicular, ring bone, or even coffin bone. I figured old Babar's hunting days might just be over.

What was I to do? I asked Nancy Miller to do more than keep an eye out for a

Babar in Retirement. Photographer: Dan Hummel, Chesapeake City, Maryland.

hunting horse. I explicitly asked her to go out and look for a suitable horse, an increasingly difficult assignment as I get older, heavier, and less agile.

Of course, for old time's sake, I called Vince. Vince knew what I was calling about. "You called on exactly the right day. It just so happens that a horse came into my stable this very morning. I said to my girls, 'Now, that's the very horse that would suit Mr. Prickett to a T if it happened he were in need. May our Lord forgive me if I did not say that very thing, don't you know? And, here, me not suspecting that you were sort of in need of just the kind of horse that came my way by pure chance this very day. Lord deliver us—it's sort of a miracle . . ."

I stopped Vince in full flight saying, "Hold hard there, Vince. This horse, whatever he is, has got to pass three tests before we even begin to talk about price."

Vince said, "Oh, and just what might they be, if I can be so bold as to inquire?"

I said, "Well, first, I've got to try him hunting. Second, he's got to vet sound. Third, Nancy Miller must approve him."

Vince said, "My, we've come a long way since Flash, haven't we, now?"

WITH THE SCARTEEN IN THE GALTEES

Oh for a horse with wings.
SHAKESPEARE, CYMBELINE

Imade two foxhunting hunting trips to Ireland. Indeed, some of my brightest memories of foxhunting are hunting with various packs in Ireland.

This is an account of hunting with one of the most famous of all Irish Masters, Thady Ryan, and his Scarteen Black & Tan Hounds. Thady was the 7th or 8th of his family to carry the horn with the Scarteen. When Thady Ryan retired, as he did some years after I was lucky enough to hunt with him, he was succeeded by his son.

I went to Ireland right after Christmas with my 16-year old stepdaughter, Mia, and her friend, Susie Peoples. Both were good riders and experienced foxhunters. What had a glorious time we had the day we went out with Thady Ryan.

After the usual thundering good breakfast at our luxurious hotel, the Cashel Palace, a Georgian house built to accommodate the needs of the Angelican Bishop of that part of Catholic Ireland, we were off at 9:30 for the little village of Ballyanders for the noon meet of the Scarteen Hunt, familiarly known as the Black & Tans. We got to the valley in which Ballyanders lies after a fairly exciting drive. Mia was at the wheel and insisted on slamming on the brakes each time we came around a corner and found a sheet of white frost on the narrow twisting country roads. She also had difficulty staying on the

Thaddy Ryan, Master of the Scarteen Hounds or the Black & Tan Hounds, February 18, 1987. Photographer: Unknown.

left side of the road. Talk about risks! Ballyanders lies in the center of a great valley surrounded by foothills beyond which rise the snow-covered Galtees Mountains, hundreds of feet high. It has one long street with four or five intersecting lanes. Upon our arrival at about 11:30, we found nobody was abroad. We wondered whether the hunt had been called off due to the heavy frost. At the pub, The Rose of Ireland, we asked Michael, the red-faced, smiling publican, if the Black & Tans were meeting. He replied, "Yank, you and your two lovely lasses be in the right place and at the right time. Thady will be right along, any minute now. Donald, there at the end of the bar in the green rubber boots, is a regular follower of the hunt, but on foot. Never misses a day, do you, Donald?" Then he added, "Will you take a thimble of poteen on the house to shrink the banks and ditches you'll be finding in our country?"

"Thanks all the same. From all we've heard, the girls and I'll need all our wits about us to follow Mr. Ryan in this country," I replied.

Michael agreed, "Good luck, Yank, and good hunting to the three of you. Come back if you've a taste for a little glass after the hunt." The regulars, including Donald of the green rubber boots, wished us well and assured us that the hunt would start right there at noon sharp.

When we left the pub, Mia said, "And just what is poteen?"

I replied, "It's Irish moonshine, untaxed potato whiskey, tastes awful, and has a terrific kick."

About 10 of 12:00, like an operetta, Main Street suddenly came alive with people, horses and hounds. Mothers with babies in prams and children came out of the houses. Old men appeared leaning on their canes, smoking their pipes. Horse "boxes" pulled by cars, tractors and trucks, rolled in. All manner of hunting horses and ponies came out or backed out of these boxes. Finally, just as the bell of the village church was striking noon, Thady Ryan and his staff appeared, beautifully turned out in pink coats, white britches and gleaming white stocks. They were mounted on fine looking horses, in contrast to the heavy but serviceable horses that we were fortunate enough to rent from Willie Gleeson, a reliable horse jobber. I rode Crow, Mia was on Jessie, and Susie was aboard Finn.

The curbs were lined with friendly onlookers. Ben Griswold, wearing his pink coat, a visiting M.F.H. from the Elkridge-Harford Hunt in Maryland, arrived with his 13-year old daughter, Nancy. Mrs. Griswold, her left leg encased in a new white knee-high cast, was hobbling with a cane. She had had a horrendous fall while hunting with the Scarteen a couple of days before. She was photographing the meet, undoubtedly wishing that she could be on the back of a good hunting horse.

Slightly after noon, and after consulting with knowledgeable local farmers, his young whips and the Scarteen regulars, Thady blew his horn "Loud and Clear" and led the hunting procession out of the village with Ben Griswold at his side. They were followed by the two whips and the bitch pack of fourteen couples of the Black & Tans. The

Thaddy Ryan, Master of the Scarteen Hounds or the Black & Tan Hounds, February 18, 1987, together with his son, Christopher, current Master of the Black & Tans. Photographer: Unknown.

hounds were followed by the mounted field of about forty. The field consisted of several hard bitten Irish foxhunters, some of whom sported thin white scars on their faces from thorn scratches, several Irish lawyers and businessmen playing hookey from professional labors, a genial priest, wearing a round collar and flapping cross, riding a black cob with a roached mane (a mane completely clipped off), a couple of grooms, jockeys and other professional horsemen. In addition, a half dozen children on ponies and small horses scampered gaily here and there, in no way daunted by the banks and ditches that would bring our hearts into our mouths. The hunting secretary gently collected the ten pound capping fee from the three of us and the other visitors. The mounted field was followed by three well behaved motorcycles and a walking field of five hearty people, including Donald. Ten cars brought up the rear. While I was delighted to have Crow as my mount again, this being his third time out in seven days, I wondered if he would hold up. (Perhaps more to the point, would I?)

When we got to the edge of town, the procession stopped while Thady cast his eager hounds down from a high bank into a smallish bog. It seemed a most unlikely place for a fox. However, proving the obvious—that Thady Ryan knew his business and I did not—in not five minutes there was a "haloo" from Donald standing on a far bank. The black and brown hounds took off, streaking lickety split, giving great tongue following a swiftly disappearing red fox. Thady Ryan was right behind the hounds. The mounted field jumped straight down the steep bank followed by some of the foot followers. The motorcycles and cars went prudently around by the roads and by ways.

Our fox led us swiftly through the bog and small field in a southwest direction away from Ballyanders, then through fields, up over large banks and over wide ditches. The members of the field were free to take their own line. At the edge of the valley, we lost Thady but followed knowledgeable Irish members of the field up, up, up into the hills. We were high above the little town and its surrounding valley, but still well below the snow-covered tops of the Galtees. Our fox then swung left. After a run of about twenty minutes in the foothills, the hounds lost the fox. Thady called the hounds to him and said, "Our fox has slipped back down into the valleys and scampered to the safety of his bog. Pity that!"

Suddenly a fox appeared. We pounded back down the road to the bog. Was this our fox or a second one? Thady stayed on the other side of the bog. Soon the hounds came out that way. The field (including the motorcycles) hurdled back up the road again, around the bog and across the floor of the valley and over some barways. At this point, we parted company with the non-jumping motorcycles. Then, with a frank jump over naked barbed wire, out we went on a great clockwise circular sweep of the hills with the steeple of Ballylanders at the center of the dial. Mia and Susie were well up with the hard riding Irish.

Someone had once told me that the right way to negotiate an Irish bank is to slow down to a walk (or even stop), allow the horse to gather itself on its hocks and leap cat-like up the bank or even right onto the very top of the bank, pause to take a look, change leads if necessary and then push resolutely off from the top after picking the right spot to land. "Momentum and speed," I was warned, "are unnecessary and may be dangerous though exhilarating."

I agreed with this analysis at the time, but I now tested and proved the soundness of what had been so wisely counseled. The hounds were flying on ahead to the west, the fox having turned back towards Ballyanders and the familiar bog. I was following Mia onto a high bank at full tilt. Jessie agilely jumped to the top of the bank and then paused an instant and jumped cleanly down the other side. Crow, with my ignorant encouragement, never paused but also jumped, just as Jessie had done, right up into the bank. His momentum carried him to the top and over, where he slipped and went in the ditch. I flew straight on for a while, but eventually gravity extended its sway, as always, over heavy non-winged objects. Delaware's version of Icarus came down to rest in the Irish mud after several heavy bounces. This was a classic fall and was thoroughly enjoyed by those behind me. The hard riding priest paused briefly but, seeing I was all right, galloped on.

Nancy (a Christian surely) stopped, came back and said, "Sir, are you okay? Say, that was one great fall!"

I said, "Thanks, Nancy. I am in one piece."

She asked, "Shall I slide off and help you back aboard?"

I replied, "No, no, the hounds are running. Go on, I'll catch up." Fortunately, I had managed to hang onto my horse's bridle so he had not been able to go careening off with bridle and stirrups flying wildly about. While neither of us was the worse for our spectacular fall, I was somewhat the wiser. Once Crow was persuaded to take his heavy hoof with an iron horseshoe off my foot, I managed to swing back up into the saddle.

I was soon off galloping after the rest of the field. It was at this point that Susie also got ditched, so to speak. She later recounted, "Finn straddled a bank and I slid off backwards. Finn sank slowly backwards into the ditch over me. It was quite some time before we decided which was which. We both finally got soggily out of the ditch and went on, wet through but not much the worse for wear!"

Soon we were almost up with Thady Ryan. After pounding along some distance at great speed, he called out, "Hold hard. We must have overrun our fox. He made good his escape." Hounds were called in by the horn. We retraced our steps.

At this point, that Mrs. Ryan, Thady Ryan's New Zealand wife, and Mrs. Griswold caught up with the hunt in the Ryans' Land Rover. I took the opportunity to slip off Crow. I reintroduced myself to Mrs. Ryan. "You may not recognize me because of my new mustache."

She seemed genuinely delighted to see me again and asked, "Would all three of you come to tea following the hunt?" Mrs. Ryan was just as grand as ever.

After a brisk trot to another high hillside, the hounds were put in a likely covert by Thady and hunted through it. This time, somewhat to our surprise, it was blank—no fox. We then went down into a boggy cover with nasty high and narrow banks in another valley. Some of those banks had half hidden semi-taunt wire, not a foot above the ground on the banks to prevent the cattle from going up onto the banks. Several of the horses were briefly snarled up in the wire.

At 4:00 p.m., the shadows were lengthening. We had already enjoyed a good hard day of fine sport but Thady was determined to show Ben Griswold, the visiting Master, even more sport. At a crossroad, Thady said, "Let's try one more covert, shall we now?" All but six foxhunters demurred, thanking Thady for a fine day of hunting and turned toward home.

The whips grumbled good naturedly, "Lord Almighty, Thady is a hard man to satisfy, now, that's the Lord's own truth!" Left were Thady, Mr. Griswold, Nancy Griswold, and me and, of course, the two whips.

Susie explained, "Jessie is plumb tired and I'm wet through and cold." Mia agreed.

As I jogged down the road I thought it was probably a mistake to go on: Crow seemed a bit tired, and I was exhausted. It was getting cold, and soon it would be dark. There was no reason to believe that there would be another fox or any further sport this evening. However, it never occurred to me to stop.

The six of us jogged south of Ballyanders down the hard road. We turned in a country road followed by two faithful motorcycles and several determined cars. The hounds were put in: surely to another blank but, no, no, no, by dunder! Suddenly there was another beautiful red fox not fifty feet away running hard just ahead of the lead hounds, with the rest of the pack streaming after in full cry. We were running flat out, clockwise across the valley. Nancy, her flaxen pigtails flying, was pressing hard on Thady. We went over all sorts of obstacles: barriers, gates, deep ditches, and banks with wire on the near side. We even jumped down from banks onto dirt roads with barbed wire on the far side. Nothing was stopping the hounds who could still be heard on ahead; nothing stopped us. After going quite a distance cross country, we came out on a hard road. We cantered along it until we came to a country lane leading straight into the foothills with the Galtees high, high above us.

Up the lane we galloped, through farm yards and across a pelting mountain stream bringing the water down from the snow covered Galtees above. We went higher still on the twisting lane, now above the level of the highest cottage. Then we jumped over a ruined gate and continued up, up toward the high sheep pastures. We went through the sheep pastures and higher still until we were in the lowest level of the mountain itself. There was snow on the ground. The hounds were still far ahead of us, and we could hear them baying as they headed toward a pass in the mountains. I had no time to look back at the staggering view of southwest Ireland stretching all the way up to Limerick itself. By this time, following the good example of the Master, we were alternately walking and trotting our tired horses. Not only had they run foxes all over the valley all afternoon but now had climbed almost straight up to better than 2,000 feet.

Finally, we came to the very end of the sheep pastures. We were at a shoulder of the mountain given over to a reforestation of Norway spruce seedlings. We went carefully through the gate in the wire fence, put there to keep the grazing sheep away from the new trees. Then we cantered on and on. Some country people walking on this snowy mountain road told us the hounds had passed that way a quarter of an hour or so earlier. So we cantered briskly up the snowy road through the fading light. Far ahead and some-

William Prickett. Photographer: Luigi Ciuffetelli, Wilmington, Delaware.

where high in this forest of little trees, we heard the hounds, still tracking their fox. We pressed on cantering or trotting upward in the fading evening light. Eventually, we caught up with three and a half couple of the hounds.

Thady was afraid if his hounds went all the way over the mountain to Fermoy, he would never see some of them again. Reluctantly, he pulled out his cold copper horn, sounding recall. He remarked between calls, "I hate to have to call my hounds off their life work of pursuing this good stout fox. It's very hard indeed to get the hounds to mind when they are on the line of a fox." The sun had now set behind the dark clouds, casting a last golden light over the wintry landscape and the checkerboard pattern of the tiny fields stretched out below. Here and there lights from cottages in the valley came on in the growing darkness. The snow-covered woods were almost completely silent. The only sound was the glorious sound of a few of the still determined Black & Tans, baying like Hiberian Bernards in the green-blue forest, punctuated by Thady's horn sounding recall again and again and again, interspersed with his piercing voice calls that made the mountainsides ring and echo.

As darkness set in, a crescent moon came up and anxiously peered down on the tired but fulfilled little group of foxhunters: the Master, the hard riding whips, Ben Griswold, Nancy and me. From far below came the sound of bells—Angelus, no doubt from a country church in one of the valleys that now lay in almost total darkness below.

Crow was much refreshed by the check and was greedily alternating between mouthfuls of cold snow and the green mountain grass he found growing below the snow itself. One of the whips went even higher to persuade the diehard hounds that they had done enough that day. Ben Griswold went in the other direction, urging other hounds to return to their beloved Master. Each tail-wagging hound received an affectionate welcome by name from Thady as well as a kind word or a soft pat as he leaned down from his saddle. Finally, we had all but one and a half couples. We made our way slowly back guided by the still watchful moon and a friendly shepherd and his dog, the horn calling now and again to the hounds still hunting in the frozen black night above us. At one point, we had to jump a bank in the dark. Crow did as well by moonlight as by sunlight.

Finally, we reached the level of the hills and were greeted by the surprised stares and friendly murmured greetings of the farmers and their families. The furious barking of the farm cur dogs showed that they at least thought that anything descending from the cold darkness at that time of night represented a threat to them, their masters and the homestead.

When we reached the hard road, a clutch of Land Rovers was waiting to welcome us back to civilization. In the headlights, I caught sight of Donald's green boots. This was Nancy's quiet moment. "You really missed it," she said to those who had gone in earlier. Soon we were jogging easily back to the horse boxes. Then I slid off Crow.

I drove the Griswolds' Land Rover with all the youngsters into Ballyanders. Once we got there, I popped all of them into the warm lounge of The Rose of Ireland, applying heat and hot chocolate to them. Michael greeted me warmly, "Welcome back Yank. Donald here told us that Thady showed you a bit of sport today. He said you stayed to the very end. Well done, Lad! Now, I am sure you won't again refuse a thimble of poteen or whatever you like. You're a guest of the house this night."

I replied, "I've never had such a day of hunting in my life. I wish I could hunt behind Thady Ryan forever. I accept with pleasure your offer of a drink. But, could I have a pint of Guiness first? I am parched and that's a fact!"

"That you may, and as many more after that one, til your thirst be quenched," said Michael pulling on the handle of his beer tap and filling a pint glass of rich dark golden brown ale topped with swirling white foam. As he handed me the Guiness, Michael said, "Donald, when he walked in, swallowed two pints, one right after the other, is that not a fact, Donald?"

Donald replied, "Deed it is. Yank, you and your two girls did yourselves proud this day."

"Thanks Donald. Now, Michael, could I have a shot of Hennessey rather than poteen? Poteen would knock me off my feet!"

"Of course, here you be," said Michael, giving me a brimming shot glass of brandy.

I turned around and addressed the whole pub, "Here's a health to Thady Ryan, to the Black & Tans, and to Ireland. Michael, fill the glasses all around so those who have a mind to can join me in that toast."

Eventually, while sallying forth to pick up still another Black & Tan hound reported walking his solitary moonlit way home, I found Mia and Susie.

As we compared notes while rushing back to the Cashel Palace to make dinner which ended at 8:30, we all agreed that it had been a fabulous day of hunting. After dinner and another couple of stiff brandies, it seemed even better. I was happy to forego the possible pleasures of a local Irish dance (or hooli) in a nearby dance hall, but the girls sallied forth for a night of Irish social life. The anxious moon now seemed content and bathed the quiet countryside below the hill of Cashel in golden moonlight.

In my dreams, which came early that night, large molasses and coffee-colored hounds climbed to the very heavens, while Crow and I soared after them, leaving all earthly cares behind.

SCARLET IF CONVENIENT

Costly your habit as your purse can buy.
SHAKESPEARE, SHAKESPEARE

People often wonder why foxhunters wear such absurd clothes. Foxhunters wear derbies and even top hats. Worse still, they wear red coats. (By tradition, the red coats are called pink coats: I don't know why.) Around their necks, they wear an elaborately tied white scarf. This outlandish dress makes present day foxhunting look like something out of an 18th Century foxhunting print. In fact, foxhunting clothes put a lot of people off because they look so pretentious.

Before I became addicted to foxhunting, I was also put off by the dress. But let me try to explain the clothes as best I can. First of all, many active foxhunters do not wear the traditional black or red coat. There are many foxhunters who dress informally. But some people who start out wearing ski parkas end up in traditional hunting clothing. On the other hand, Ralph Reeber, the most avid foxhunter I know, who hunts his own farmer's pack of American hounds with his brothers, cousins and friends all through the valleys of the White Clay Creek, usually hunts in a ski parka.

First, the hats. Originally, foxhunters wore top hats. Why? Because these hats afforded the best protection then known to the head of the rider when he took a fall. The top hat was not perfect protection especially since it often came off in a fall. Additionally, if the top hat did stay on, a badly fitting top hat was often pushed down in a fall, its edges cutting the rider's ears, and sometimes breaking the wearer's nose. Still, that was better than cracking one's bean on hard ground.

The bowler or derby was an improvement. If firmly placed on the head, the rounded shape of a hard crowned bowler hat afforded better protection. Still, it left something to be desired. Head injuries were still common. The padded caliente helmet (named, I believe, after the race course where it originated) with a chin strap used

William Prickett on Tug. Photographer: Unknown.

originally by race riders and show riders was slowly and somewhat grudgingly permitted in the hunting field. There are foxhunters who, disdaining the added safety of a caliente helmet, still wear a bowler or, with a pink coat, a top hat. However, when all is said and done, the caliente helmet is clearly the thing to wear since falls are inevitable. A fall on the head can result in a head injury, but it is less apt to happen with a caliente helmet.

You might well ask "Why, for goodness sake, do people still wear black coats or red coats? To outsiders, it looks kind of silly in this day and age."

Actually, the black hunting coat is a very practical garment when you come right down to it. It is usually made of heavy wool which keeps the foxhunter warm on cold winter days and dry in all but a real downpour. A hunting coat extends down well below the belt line to keep the rider warm around his middle. Finally, a wool coat is easy to keep clean since a good stout brushing removes mud and horse sweat.

The red coat is traditionally called a pink coat. The pink coat is, of course, traditional, but it also serves a practical function. The hunting staff—the Huntsman and his whips—are usually dressed in pink coats during the foxhunting season. The Master of Foxhounds and the Field Master also usually wear pink coats. These coats are visible not only from a great distance but also through the woods and on hilltops. This enables the Huntsman, for example, to spot the position of his eyes and ears—his whips, and vice versa. It also enables the Master of Foxhounds or the Field Master, who is restraining but leading the field, to see just where the Huntsman is and where he is going so that the Master or the Field Master can keep the field up without getting in the way. Thus, in a word, the continued use of the pink coat—at least for the hunting staff, the Master and the Field Master—allows them to be seen clearly across the hills, fields and in the woods.

Foxhunters well turned out in pink coats add color. Certainly, foxhunting has strong elements of drama and pageantry. Thus, the addition of pink coats in the field adds color, history and romance to hunting. It certainly is a stirring sight to see a well mounted rider with shined boots in a pink coat, a clean white stock with a gold pin in it and a hat that is not covered with mud. No doubt about it, Mrs. Hannum (like most Masters) takes pride in the fact that her field is well turned out and does not look like a collection of gypsies, horse rustlers or roofers!

Unfortunately, what I have been talking about is a standard which I have never measured up to. Certainly, no one has ever accused me of being sartorially splendid. When I first started hunting, I was young lawyer and I did not have the funds for fancy new riding clothes or boots. Instead, I scrounged articles from Harry the Gyp, an old Irishman who drove around to the various hunts in a battered station wagon with piles of old hunting clothes and boots that he bought from, I guess, estates of deceased foxhunters. I got my first pair of black boots from him. They were, when shined, marginally presentable. I also bought a pair of hunting coats from him. The most memorable one was an ancient Shad belly coat that provoked guffaws from my fellow foxhunters each time I wore it. Indeed, I looked like something out of Jorrocks (the comic hero of a 19th Century collection of English foxhunting stories). These old coats, however, served me well for years. I think I still have the Shad belly somewhere in our cedar closet. The other wore out and literally came to pieces on the thorns of the hedges of Ireland and had to be discarded. I, at that point, had a tough, serviceable wool coat made in Tipperary, Ireland. It served me well for years. Finally, my girth became such that I simply could not button it. Thus, I went about flapping like a black crow on a winter day. Recently, I bought another black coat that I trust will see me to the end of my hunting days.

"What about stocks?" Originally, I believe that the stock was a form of necktie of the time. Beyond the fact that it was ornamental, the stock served a real purpose then and serves that same purpose occasionally even today. Since a stock is about two and one-half feet long, it can serve as a bandage or a sling or to help splint a leg temporarily. I have used a stock to immobilize the leg of a fallen foxhunter that was obviously broken, until the injured foxhunter could be loaded into the back of a station wagon and taken to the hospital. I have often seen a stock used as a temporary sling for a broken collarbone. One of my stocks was ruined when I offered it to a small child who had had a fall and had a bloody nose. But normally, a stock is simply an ornamental and traditional bit of hunting clothing.

How ornamental a stock is depends somewhat on who ties it. In all these years, I myself have never really gotten the knack of tying a stock so that it flares out properly. In my younger years, I tied my stock as I was driving furiously down to Middletown, Delaware, to join the Vicmead hounds. An old foxhunter who was always impeccably turned out once described my stock as looking like a dirty dishrag around the neck of a terrier. I was quite embarrassed. Thereafter, I made sure my stock was always clean. I still have trouble tying my stock properly, though countless well-meaning foxhunters have patiently sat down and shown me just how to do it and just where to put the pin. Over the years, I have been given stock pins as presents in the form of whips, foxes, hounds and stirrups, some gold filled and others sterling silver. Because I invariably pull my stock off at the end of a hard hunt, I inevitably lost these fancy stock pins. Fortunately, when my daughter, Annie, was born, there was a ready supply of diaper pins with blue plastic ends which I pressed into service for a couple of years. I now buy packets of fifty safety pins and use them one by one, not regretting when I lose one.

Some people, particularly the ladies, even after the hardest hunt, remain impeccable: they are neat and tidy when they dismount, with their hair and stock still in place and as clean as when they mounted their horses. Somehow they end up with very little mud on their boot and coats. I, on the other hand, attract mud. Thus, even on a clear dry day, I am apt to come in with mud splattered on my boots, breeches and coat, and on my stock.

When hounds are flying and high fences come frequently, nobody really looks to see whether your stock is properly tied and pinned. Years ago, I used to simply step out of my hunting clothes, take a shower, and then go right on to my next pleasure. That meant that the following Saturday there was always a mad scramble to round up a complete set of hunting clothes that was presentable enough to keep them from being sent out of the hunting field. I have learned my lesson. Now, no matter how tired I am or how pressing my next engagement is, I religiously clean my boots, brush my coat, and put a fresh set of white gloves in the pocket of my hunting coat. I put a clean shirt and stock together with clean hunting breeches so that all I have to do is grab my hunting clothes on the way out of the house.

My first pink coat came from Mike the Gyp, who turned up one time with a beautiful old English-made pink coat which I instantly bought. I proudly squeezed myself into it. It was made of indestructible, fine English woolen cloth. However, my taste for food and beer eventually led to the inevitable result that I simply could no longer get into the coat nor have it let out any more. I reluctantly gave it away to a slimmer member of the hunting staff: I believe it is still being used on cold days. I hankered for another pink coat, but my Presbyterian miserliness prohibited me from going out and just plain buying one since they are monstrously expensive, particularly if custom made by an English tailor.

The color of the collar of a hunting coat, whether black or pink, is a sign of the hunt to which the member belongs. After a foxhunter has been seasoned and is found to be acceptable, the Master may award him or her their "colors." Usually the actual award is in the form of the presentation of a hunt button. This entitles the foxhunter to wear the colors of the hunt. This means the hunter has the right to put a colored collar on one's hunting coat and substitute a set of hunt buttons for plain buttons on the hunting coat. Mr. Stewart's Cheshire Foxhounds in Unionville, however, is a private pack as contrasted with a subscription pack. There are no colors, and the members hunt without colored collars.

There is one other thing or privilege that comes from having been awarded colors: that is, the right to wear a scarlet tail coat at hunt balls.

Thus, the title of this chapter is the phrase, "Scarlet If Convenient." The title refers to what foxhunters wear at hunt balls and appears on the bottom of an invitation to a hunt ball.

I came home the other night and found a heavy envelope addressed to me in beautiful script handwriting. I opened it: there was an engraved invitation to the Annual Hunt Ball. A notation below the R.S.V.P. in the lower left hand corner discreetly said "Scarlet If Convenient."

As I looked at the invitation, the notation "Scarlet If Convenient" brought back a flood of memories. Indeed, a carefully cleaned scarlet coat is hanging downstairs in my sweet smelling cedar closet. It was and is a beautifully garment "built" by Dege & Son, an English tailor who proudly announces that Dege has a patent to the Queen Mother (whatever that is). One of the many reasons why I try ineffectually to keep my weight down is to be able to fit into this handsome garment once a year or so.

However, I get ahead of myself. It was not always that way. Before taking up foxhunting in my early thirties, I had never been to a ball where the foxhunters dressed in their beautiful scarlet coats with white facings and colored collars that identified the hunt of the wearer. After a couple of years with the Vicmead, I was awarded my "colors." This meant that I was entitled to adorn my somber black hunting coat with the dark Lincoln

Invitation to the Masters Ball with notation "Scarlet if convenient."

You are cordially invited to attend

The Masters Ball,

a dinner dance,

on Friday, January twenty-seventh

nineteen hundred and eighty-four

The Grand Ballroom

The Pierre

Fifth Avenue at Sixty-first Street, New York City

Lester Lanin's Orchestra

Scarlet, if convenient $75.00 per person
Cocktails at 7:30   Please make reservations
Dinner served promptly at 8:30   prior to January 20

green collar of the Vicmead Hunt. It also meant that I could, if I had the means, sport a scarlet (note: not pink) tail coat at hunt balls. But I did not have the $500 or $600 that it took to have one of these handsome coats built (to use the English tailor's lingo again). Thus, I went to hunt balls dressed in a somber black tuxedo, green with envy at my fellow foxhunters in their these flashy scarlet Tanniger coats. I was sure that my success with the debutante crowd would increase markedly if I could strut about in such an outfit even though I was awkward as Icabod Crane in terms of social graces: my dancing was basically, and still is, the Delaware two-step. (That was all my mother and old Mrs. Clafferty, the dancing teacher, were able to teach me.)

Then a friend stepped in. His deceased father had had three of these coats built. To make a long story short, my friend one time generously asked me if I would like to borrow one of these coats for the upcoming Vicmead Ball. I accepted with alacrity. All too soon, it got to be the regular thing: I would call up and haltingly arrange to borrow a scarlet coat, wear it, then have it cleaned and return it for storage in my friend's cedar closet.

One night, I was driving back to home to Corner Ketch, Delaware, after a particularly "happy" ball in Maryland wearing my borrowed finery. I usually took off the coat and drove home in a raincoat or my shirt sleeves. But on this occasion, I had piled into my battered station wagon wearing the scarlet coat. At some point in the evening, I had picked up a paper admiral's hat, and I still had that on my head. An empty champagne glass lay on the seat beside me. As I was zipping along, I saw to my horror in my rear view mirror the flashing red lights of a Delaware State Police car behind me. I was pulled over. One of the officers walked up with a flashlight. He looked inside and called to his partner: "Holy Cow, I don't believe this! Man, come over and take a look. We've got ourselves a real classic!"

Together, they stood there in awe: there was the perfect picture of someone who should not be driving. I knew that I had been caught dead to rights. There was no possibility of piously saying that I had had only the traditional two beers, or something equally implausible. To make a long story short, they were so amused, and I was so contrite (and actually sober), that they warned me to drive very carefully right on home. I felt like a felon who had bent his head down on the block and found the guillotine knife was made of rubber.

Well, to get back to my story, I did not mind borrowing a scarlet coat a couple of times, nor did my friend mind lending me one, but I really hankered after my very own scarlet coat. However, my wages at my father's Presbyterian law firm did not permit even thoughts of such sartorial extravagance.

One day, I happened to be in New York in a hotel room, waiting for a telephone call. Idly flipping through the yellow pages, I come to an entry that said "Men's Evening Wear." There were a dozen advertisements for fancy tuxedos for the theatrical trade. One ad proclaimed that Henry Rosen could and would make tuxedos of any color. I dialed Mr. Rosen's telephone number: the guarded voice was none other than of Henry Rosen himself. I told him that what I needed was not a tuxedo coat but a tail coat. Mr. Rosen said, "Of course. I know vhat you need and I vould be happy to do it for you."

I said, "But I want the coat in red with white facings and a green collar."

Mr. Rosen replied, "Wow! I ain't never had to make one that way with dos colors. Say, what are you? An animal trainer, a magician or what?"

"No," I replied somewhat loftily. "I am a foxhunter."

"Well," Mr. Rosen replied somewhat uncertainly, "det don't make no difference at all. It's none of my damn business, but me and the girls can certainly make dat kind of a coat. Vat color are the pants going to be?"

I said, "I don't need any pants." (Of course, I was going to wear my regular tuxedo pants.)

Mr. Rosen whistled and said, "I never heard of a guy who only needs a red coat and don't need no pants." Mr. Rosen didn't seem to understand at all.

Nevertheless, I took a taxi to the garment district and found his building. Mr. Rosen's tailoring loft was on the 7th floor. I rode the freight elevator up and got off. There was a big heavy iron door with Mr. Rosen's name on it. I rang the bell. A tiny peephole opened and Mr. Rosen looked me carefully over. He then opened the heavy door and welcomed me in his establishment as a long lost friend (albeit of only an hour). He was a small fat man with a nice smile. He was wearing slippers and a black old vest with pins stuck in all over it. On his head was a small yarmulke. He had a yellow tape measure around his neck. His little eyes twinkled behind his small glasses which were perched on the very edge of his large nose. I clearly had come to the right place: the loft was full of racks of marching band costumes and brightly colored tuxedos. Mr. Rosen told me his specialty was making tuxedos for jazz bands, but he occasionally make up outfits for actors, circus performers, lion tamers and musicians.

I repeated, "What I need is a red tail coat." Henry (we were already on a first name basis) pulled out a package with some red material. Under the artificial light, the red seemed suitable. The facing material of white rayon also seemed right. The green for the collar, while not truly the dark Lincoln green of the Vicmead, also seemed okay. I told Henry that I would need brass buttons. He replied gravely, "Bill, that vill have to be an extra: thirty-one cents each." I told him that I would spring for the brass buttons.

Henry then asked, "Ven vuld you be needing this fancy coat?"

I replied loftily, "I need it for the Maryland Hunt Cup Ball in about two weeks."

He shook his head doubtfully and then cheerfully said, "Den dis has got to be one hell of a hurry-up order." He quietly added to himself, "I'll get Rosa to get right to work on the coat. Because you are coming to be an old friend of the establishment, I am sure ve can get it done. Ve will send it directly down to Maryland." He nudged me and said, "No charge for the mailing. How about that?"

He first checked the label in the pocket of my suit coat for my size. He then took a couple of measurements with the yellow tape hanging around his neck.

After paying him and thanking him, I left Henry's loft with a light heart, pleased with myself. For a very modest sum, I had aced the expensive English tailors and their built coats and would now have my very own scarlet coat. Two weeks later, I went down to Maryland and fetched up with a friend and his wife. Yes, indeed, there was a heavy brown paper package from 7th Avenue waiting for me. After the race, I took out my Swiss army knife and cut the heavy brown twine and opened the package. In the Maryland afternoon sunlight, the coat did not look quite as fine as the materials had looked in New York under the florescent lights of the loft. The red was not at all right. The white facing had the look and feel of a cheap rayon slip. The collar was a bright Kelly green instead of the somber Lincoln green of the Vicmead. The brass buttons at thirty-one cents apiece looked just about like that. Still, ignorance is bliss. I was not about to cavil about the quality of my new coat. My friends, who had inherited coats of the finest quality from generations of fathers, uncles and great uncles, were highly amused.

I showed up at the ball in this outlandish piece of finery to the amusement of one and all. Nevertheless, I was having a fine time and didn't very much care that the older stuffed shirts harumphed when they saw this obviously cheap copy of the proper regalia. But I happened to run into a very senior member of the Vicmead Hunt. He looked impeccable in a finely built scarlet coat with proper buttons, studs and a crisp stiff shirt. I could tell that he was horrified. He said quietly to me, "If you are going to wear scarlet, you ought at least to do it properly." He then said, "The next time Dege, the tailor, comes to Wilmington, for God's sake, go and get fitted out with a decent scarlet coat and throw that abomination that you are wearing into the nearest ash can."

I did as I was told. After three fittings over two years, my proper scarlet coat seemed entirely ready to me. I was all for wearing it right away, but the English tailor insisted on a final fitting: "My goodness, our left shoulder does not fit just exactly right, now does it?"

Of course, little did he know the tough rigors that this coat was going to have to undergo from then on. I was not one to worry about whether there is a little crease or wrinkle here or there. Nevertheless, the tailor firmly insisted on getting the coat just right. The proper Vicmead buttons were L5 per button (or a total of $45.00, about half of what my 7th Avenue coat had cost). After three years, my scarlet coat was finally done, and I was then smartly turned out for the next foxhunting function.

As noted above, there are all sorts of other things that go along with a scarlet coat, including a starched stiff shirt with a detachable wing collar and a white vest that requires three special little buttons.

Years ago as a third former at Kent School, I had to struggle Sunday after Sunday getting the required stiff collar on for Chapel. Those juvenile efforts now paid off: I could assemble the whole white tie rig with fair ease. But, I always had difficulty in keeping track of all the paraphernalia: studs, collar buttons, cufflinks, collar and white tie. One time I was asked to the Master of Foxhounds' Ball in New York. I was staying at the Knickerbocker Club and found to my horror that when I was all dressed and ready to sally forth that I had somehow forgotten to include a white tie. I could get a black tie from one of the staff of the Club, but where in the world could I get a white tie at 8:00 o'clock on a Saturday night in midtown New York? However, "necessity is the mother of invention": I found a heavy linen towel in the bathroom about a foot-and-a-half long. With my little scissors on my Swiss Army knife, I laboriously cut off a two-inch strip. I put it around my collar and made the required bow tie out of it. It was generally remarked that night that for once my white tie really looked about right. I took the balance of the towel home and cut off a new tie whenever I needed one. I have often thought of going back to that club to replenish my supply.

Recently, I went to the Unionville Foxhunting Ball. As I brought out my lovely scarlet coat, I noticed a pair of bib overalls on a hanger in the closet. As a sartorial lark, I decided to wear my bib overalls under my scarlet coat and over my tuxedo trousers, at least for a little while. Everyone was amused, but one Boston blueblood was horrified. He said with a haughty sniff, "You are a disgrace to your colors. If you were a member of our field, I would see to it that you were immediately stripped of your colors."

I was about to reply in kind, telling him plainly that he was not in his field, but a guest, and therefore he ought to mind his manners and get himself some sense of humor. Caroline, my spouse, who had heard what he had said and had seen the veins in the back of my neck swell up, put her arm gently on my scarlet sleeve and said, "My dear, may I have this dance?"

Scarlet is now convenient, but the trail to get there was not convenient at all.

FEBRUARY 11, 1988

The Outside of a Horse is Good for the Inside of a Man.
OLD PROVERB

Even though I love foxhunting, in terms of time spent, it has really been a very small part of my life. Like my father, and grandfather, as well as my only son, I am a lawyer, and, again, like most lawyers, I am always frantically busy. Therefore, I have only been able to go hunting on Saturdays and holidays in the fall, the winter and the early spring. In addition to my legal life and foxhunting, I am, like everybody else, interested in all manners of different things. I have an account of a Saturday a number of years ago.

At the time, I was rereading James Joyce, so, of course, I set all this day's events down, sort of trying to reflect the approach found in *Ulysses*. I know that I blaspheme. I saw how hard it is to write like Joyce and what a great master he really is. His writing is truly four-dimensional; whereas, this account is plainly one-dimensional, or perhaps non-dimensional.

I was awakened by the clapper striking the biggest bell seven times in the belfry of nearby Immanuel Church which was only a block away from the house I was renting at 53 The Strand, New Castle.

I rolled over and gazed out of my bedroom window and across the second floor porch. There, on the frost covered lawn stood my statue of Poseidon at the far edge of the garden atop the two giant millstones. Down across the New Castle Common, at the very edge of the Delaware River, stood a row of rusty iron pilings, part of the ruins of the old New Castle Yacht Basin. My concrete statue of Pocahontas stood at the edge of the Common, waving greeting to passing ships and mariners. Out on the gray waters of the polluted Delaware River stood the ancient snow white stone ice breakers capped by a solemn row of gray gulls. Beyond the shimmering oily waters of the Delaware was the low

Jack Trainer going over a stiff fence. Photographer: James Graham, Montchanin, Delaware.

Jersey shore, just emerging from the early morning haze. The sickly winter sun, the pale yellow of a supermarket egg yolk, was reluctantly rising in the east above the Jersey shoreline.

A loaded tanker labored slowly up the Delaware, its pilot flag drooping in the motionless winter air. The quiet sound of the tanker's giant diesel motors could be heard humming across the water from a mile away. A tiny wisp of smoke came lazily out of the tanker's black stack. This oil-ladenleviathan slowly disappeared under the twin Memorial Bridges linking Delaware to New Jersey. As I lay there for an additional minute, a tiny tug pulling a large barge, like an ant dragging a large bread crumb, appeared under the bridges going downriver ever so slowly southward.

I was tired and was glad I had slept through, til 7 o'clock. I was also dejected: nothing had been going right. I had been in an important corporate trial all that week in the Delaware Court of Chancery, working in Court from the unusually early hour of 9:00 a.m. until well past 5:00 p.m., cross-examining hostile witnesses and responding to the meritless objections of a pair of very tiresome New York lawyers, both of whom fancied themselves as Delaware corporate litigators. The Court had not brought sufficient discipline to the trial but allowed them and (I guess, to be fair, me) to go on and on. Though I had the able assistance of another partner, each night I myself had had to prepare myself until all hours for the next day's session.

In addition, I had a dozen pressing collateral matters, some of which were

Jack Trainer and Cheshire Field going over a stiff fence. Photographer: James Graham, Montchanin, Delaware.

101

troubling, including a couple of important cases and a meritless malpractice suit against a member of the firm. In addition, I was a member of a committee to consider and recommend yet another necessary addition to our complex of law office buildings. I remembered that I had promised to drop by Andy and Betsy Wyeth's house late Saturday afternoon to go over the proposed IBM contract. Beyond that, I faced mounting problems stemming from my separation and divorce. Indeed, my divorce was the reason why I found myself in New Castle rather than in Greenville, Delaware. I was troubled because I had never persuaded Annie to come out foxhunting with me. I thought glumly that in all likelihood I never would. I knew she would like it if she just tried it. I hated to think that Annie would go through life without ever having even tasted the pleasures and excitement of foxchasing. More importantly, I thought if we could just spend our Saturday afternoons together on horseback, we would have something in common for all time to come.

I lay back for an additional few minutes and thought back on all the disappointing events of the past week. Still, the week at the office had come to an end on a mini high note: I had joined in a farewell beer at the end of the day for a paralegal who was leaving the firm to take a better paralegal job at a corporation. I could not blame her at all. All the same, I was sorry since she was an efficient and pleasant person.

Friday night had been also fun: perhaps too much so. I had showered, changed my shirt, and driven out to Centerville, Delaware, to a dinner party. When I got there, I found that, besides myself, there was a most pleasant group of old friends. After drinks, dinner was announced. There was a really good soup followed by an equally fine dinner with French wine. Afterwards, we had coffee in the living room. I unwisely accepted the proffer of a "slug" of 1924 Prohibition applejack. It was smooth, strong and delicious, but I knew from former experiences that it had a treacherous boomerang effect. I compounded this folly by weakly acceding to a suggestion that a cold beer was just the thing to top the evening off. After a second beer, I said my goodnights. I had had a generous alcoholic evening, so I drove most carefully on home to New Castle: it had been a fun evening.

I got on home at 11 o'clock, read several pages in Joyce's *Ulysses* (Molly Bloom, lying in her bed, describes the bullfights she saw in Spain when she lived in Gibraltar), heard the twelve strokes of midnight tolled by the bell of nearby Immanuel Church and went to sleep with both my glasses and the light on and the all night classical program of WFLN playing quietly away. I awoke after 2:00, took off my glasses, turned off the light and the radio and went back to a troubled night of sleep.

Back to Saturday morning: after showering, shaving and dressing in long-johns and riding britches as well as a clean stock shirt, I pulled a pair of extra large chinos over my riding pants and boots. I gathered my canvas hunting bag with a clean stock (and a safety pin which serves as a stock pin) as well as my hunting coat, my caliente helmet and a change of shirt and an old sport coat. I went downstairs to the kitchen where I turned WFLN on. My little espresso coffee machine tempted me, but I knew that I would pay dearly later in the day if I drank even a single cup of coffee. Whenever I was going foxhunting, I wisely avoided a jolt of espresso, or indeed any coffee to save my kidneys. But,

I did indulge myself: two delicious baked eggs as well as a "smidgeon" (as my old Irish nurse, Rita, said) of the Christmas ham that my daughter, Priscilla, had sent me from Bozeman, Montana. Which I finished up with a slice of my own delicious home baked bread while I scanned the morning paper, noting in passing that the movie, *Dangerous Liaisons*, was playing at the Tri-State Mall: there was a 7:30 showing that I might well work in after seeing the Wyeths in Chadds Ford. I wrapped the remains of the homemade bread and stuck it in my hunting bag together with the last little piece of country ham and a big cold can of Foster's Australian beer.

As I was going out the door, I met my next door neighbor, a legal colleague, who was all bundled up for a cold winter's day. He had his diminutive terrier on a leash, taking her out for her brisk morning walk. She sniffed around at my boots and growled. He said, "Down, Dog. Neighbor, how is your trial going?" I was somewhat surprised that he knew that I was in a trial, but the Delaware corporate bar is a small backyard sort of community.

Leaving my colleague and his little dog to their Saturday morning walk, I drove westward to the end of the Strand and then turned right and went one block up on Delaware Avenue and into the fabulous colonial center of Old New Castle. Most of the little town was still slumbering. The only persons up and about, other than my neighbor, were a few hardy joggers and elderly stalwarts taking their early morning runs and constitutionals through Battery Park. I turned right again and went past the original State House. As I bumped along on the cobblestones of Second Street, I looked at Immanuel Church, rebuilt after it had been gutted by a fire in the 1960s, its gleaming white steeple sharply outlined against the steely blue winter sky. I realized that I had never been to a service there. Tomorrow, there would be a peal of bells from the bell tower reminding me of my days as a third former and a young bell ringer in 1940 at Kent School. What a long time ago! As I bumped slowly along the cobblestone street by the Church, I thought of my dear deceased friend, Doug Buck. His father, a governor of Delaware, was buried right here in the Immanuel Church Graveyard. I drove on down past 122 Second Street, the house of my benevolent housekeeper Marie Lewis. Reaching Route 9, I picked up my car telephone and talked to my retired nurse, Rita, now living out her days at the Hillside Nursing Home. This call was a daily ritual, ostensibly for her pleasure but really more for my pleasure. We discussed the weather and then satisfied ourselves that we were both well. We touched on each of my children, Will, a law student at Widener Law School, Priscilla married and living out West, and Annie in grade school at Tatnall School, as well as on the various dogs. I drove up the circular ramp and out onto Interstate 495. I came this way today to stare again at the blackened superstructure and hull of a freighter that had caught fire and burned spectacularly all day Thursday in spite of the concerted efforts of the whole of Wilmington's marine fire brigade, re-enforced by help from surrounding marine firefighting boats. There she was: brown and black and charred, waiting to be towed away. It had been a dramatic sight seeing her aflame on Thursday morning as I had driven up this way on my way to the office. This charred hulk carried me back to my days in the Navy when as a young seaman I had fought real, raging oil fires aboard training ships during World War II.

I came out to the Governor Printz Boulevard, stopped until early Saturday morning traffic parted, and then shot on through and drove parallel to the Brandywine in the shadows of the great towering dumps of scrap metal that lie between the Boulevard and the 12th Street Bridge over the Brandywine Creek. I turned left, went over the bridge and drove on up past the police horse stables, past the Waterworks Restaurant and turned left on French Street. I came to our parking lot and the familiar outline of our complex of brick buildings. Already, there was a scattering of six or so cars in the lot. I looked up at the end of our Washington Building, checking it to see whether I was correct that there could be a three-story addition that would include one almost subterranean story. I grabbed my briefcase and went in the back door, using the current combination of 245.

I picked up my mail and in-house documents in my mail slot in the new mailroom and walked through the basement and up the back stairs to my handsome office. I checked my voice mail: no calls. I went through my Saturday morning routine—I wound my father's grandfather clock and watered my two rubber plants. I filled out my time sheets from the day before and reviewed the duplicate copy of my diary and schedule for Monday and the coming week: trial again (Ugh!). I then reviewed all my mail, scanning it first to see if by any chance there were any long awaited opinions or checks (there were none). I went through all of the remaining mail, discarding a good deal of it while redirecting some for the attention of other attorneys and others for filing by my secretary, Mrs. Phyllis Zehr. Some went into my dictation pile. I also had a second revision of an Allied-Signal brief in support of our motion to dismiss based on "forum non conveniens." There was a newspaper from Delaware Law School. I was ready to chuck it when I noticed that the lead article was a belated announcement of Will's victorious argument in the DeBona Moot Court competition back in November. I decided to save it for inclusion in the current Prickett Family Newsletter which was about to go out. However, as I was cutting it out, I remembered that I had already included a more timely publication of this legal win by Will, so I chucked the article after all. I got a letter from my sister-in-law, Erna Prickett, enclosing a memorial to my brother, Harry, which I put aside to include in the Family Newsletter together with a copy of my little musical memoir that had been published in the *Delaware Lawyer* entitled "Wolfgang Amadeus Prickett."

I then met the managing partner, Wayne Elliott, and Richie Jones about the current malpractice lawsuit against a member of the firm. Because of my trial I had been unable to attend the Executive Committee meeting, so we wanted to meet to share thoughts on how the matter should be handled. Richie mentioned that he and his wife, Annie, would not be going out foxhunting that day because they were off to New York.

My grandfather clock was ticking away behind me, striking the hours and half hours. It was already past 10:00. I therefore restuffed my briefcase, including the draft of the IBM-Wyeth contract. I told the Saturday morning receptionist that I might come back in the late afternoon. Then I jumped back in my Jeep and backed out of our parking lot, half guilty, as always, because there was a score of things I should do rather than go foxhunting.

As I drove out Pennsylvania Avenue, I passed the Columbus Inn where I had gone as a child with Rita (to meet her boyfriend at the time, a postman), the green copper roof of Rockford Tower and the cupola of Tower Hill School from which I was expelled, past the Wilmington Country Club, and so to Greenville where I stopped at Marvi Cleaners to leave off my dirty shirts for the laundry and a suit for dry cleaning. I thought of stopping at Janssen's for a little bit of grocery shopping but, by now, it was getting on towards 10:30. I certainly did not want to miss the beginning of the hunt at 11:00 a.m. (though it was usually 11:15 before hounds actually moved off).

I drove on out the Kennett Pike, past the historic cherry tree, which Patty and Andy Hobbs had planted. It stands where George Washington is supposed to have dismounted on his way to the disastrous Battle of the Brandywine. I drove past the Route 82 intersection where the family house in Greenville is and where Annie, age 10, was probably still sleeping or perhaps watching silly Saturday morning cartoons on T.V. I wished again, as always, that Annie would try foxhunting with me rather than endlessly doing horse shows. Will, who also lived there, may have been already hard at work on his law school studies. I passed Winterthur, and the Old Brick Church where my father and my mother lie buried under the giant white oat tree behind the boxwood hedge that surrounds the family grave plot (and where I presumably will lie some day), drove down the long hill and up the other side and into Centreville.

Eventually I fetched up in Unionville. After passing through the village, I turned left and drove down into the hunting country. There, at a level spot, were Chuck Hinkson and Lin Morrow and Wendy Dixon, my stablemates at Nancy Miller's hunting barn, all impatiently waiting for the van, anxious not to be late for the start. A few moments later, Archy came zipping over the top of the hill in Nancy's familiar blue gooseneck horse van. Archy stopped behind our cars, calling out a cheery greeting. He opened the door of the van. The excited hunters, one by one, pounded down the ramp, eager as their riders to be off and about the day's business.

I pulled on my caliente helmet, buckled the strap, made doubly sure that my white cotton gloves were in my pocket. I went over to the van and took Peter the Great's reins from Arch who retightened my girth. I then found a convenient high bank that enabled me to get a stiffened left leg into the stirrup. With some help from Arch, who steadied my anxious horse, holding the right stirrup to make doubly sure the saddle did not slip around, I swung into the saddle and slipped my right foot into the stirrup. I rechecked my girth once again and made certain that the stirrups were of a proper and equal length. Already, my stabling companions were trotting briskly off up West Road, to make sure they were not left at the start of the meet. It felt great to be aboard Peter on a perfectly delicious winter day, with every prospect of getting some much needed exercise, relaxation, and good sport, leaving behind all the professional and other cares making this a particularly low period in my life. As I trotted off, Nancy Miller drove up, and Arch brought her mount for that day out of the van.

I galloped briskly up to the meet. Hounds met that day at the ancient and now long unused Walker polo field on West Road. There was the three-man hunting staff— Gerald, the English Huntsman, the red-bearded, long time Saturday whip, Larry Snyder, and my old friend from Vicmead days, Monk Crossan, son of Oscar Crossan all immaculately turned out in polished black boots with gleaming spurs, pink coats and snowy white breeches. They wore black hunting caps with, by long tradition, the ribbons in the back hanging down rather than being sewn up on the cap itself. Some of the hounds were clustered around the Huntsman looking adoringly up at Gerald. Others were quietly playing among themselves or scratching imaginary fleas while waiting for Gerald's horn to sound, signaling the start of the day's hunt.

In the meanwhile, Mrs. Hannum, the Master of Foxhounds, Gerald, as well as Bruce Davidson, the Field Master that day, and his wife, Mrs. Hannum's daughter, Carol, and several others were listening to Mrs. Hannum as she laid out the day's plan and the hunting strategy. From various directions, other members of the field came trotting up by two's and three's. There were, I guess, 45 or 50 people when we moved off shortly after 11:00 a.m. Contrary to what many people believe, foxhunting, at least in the Cheshire Country, is democratic. Anyone with decent manners, a sound hunting horse, the courage and ability to face an occasional stiff fence, and who is reasonably pleasant, is welcomed by Mrs. Hannum as well as the field, particularly if the person in question has a serious interest (as opposed to a social interest) in foxhunting. There is no drinking at all before the meet, at the meet, or during the hunt. (Not quite true: occasionally, a small flask may be passed about as the field jogs homeward after a long hard day. There are not a few foxhunters, myself among them, who do not refuse and may indeed welcome a couple of swallows following a long hard day.)

The group that gathered that Saturday morning was typical of the diverse, hard riding field of the Cheshire though somewhat smaller than on previous winter Saturdays since the New Year because many students had gone back to school. No children were going out, probably due to the cold weather. The T.V. and radio weather prediction, generally wrong, called for a very cold but clear winter day. Since it was not very cold, I was glad not to have put on a down vest under my black wool hunting coat.

At about ten after 11:00, Gerald pulled the short copper horn from between the second and third button of his pink coat and blew a series of staccato musical blasts on it. As the hounds packed up behind him, he trotted off in a generally westerly direction down the road. We fell in behind the Field Master, in two's and three's. At the edge of the cover or woods, the hounds were cast by Gerald into the leafless wintery woods. We could see them streaming through the trees and undergrowth, sniffing and snuffing this way and that to the sound of the encouraging but unintelligible words that Huntsmen have used for centuries and only hounds (and perhaps foxes) understand. Gerald also gave an occasional blast on his copper horn. The two whips had posted themselves well out on the flanks to halloo if they spotted a fox sliding out of the woods and loping away.

The first cast in the woods produced nothing: it was blank. Crossing the road, we traversed the old polo field and searched into the woods on the far side, again blank. We had, in the meanwhile, come to a couple of small fences. To my embarrassment, Peter the Great stumbled over the first. At the second fence, he stopped and then stepped delicately over it. Clearly, Peter was not yet awake. Pretty soon we came to a tricky three-foot fence next to a stout gate, and Peter pricked his ears up and went handily over it. After that, he would either cleanly sail over them or gracefully tuck his large feet to the left and slide over the fences with minimal effort.

At about 11:30, the hounds opened; they were on to a fox. There was the stentorian hallo echoing across the countryside from a distant hilltop. Mrs. Hannum was out of her blue Jeep and had viewed the fox. Indeed, a beautiful tawny orange fox was viewed in the distance. Hounds were lifted and led to the place where the fox had last been seen. To everyone's disappointment, the scent of the fox, that mysterious quality that spells the difference between success and failure for a foxhunt, just was not there for some unknowable reason. The hounds could do very little in spite of Gerald's expert casting and recasting of the pack.

We then trotted on over to another cover. I glanced at my watch: it was 1:00. The Texaco Saturday afternoon broadcast of Verdi's great opera about Phillip, II's son, *Don Carlos*, would be just getting underway. I would have liked to listen to it since I was going to see and hear it at the Metropolitan Opera with my sister, Elise, and her husband, Bobby, on Thursday, the 23rd of February. Perhaps I would catch the latter half of the opera over my car radio after hunting was over.

As the hounds went through the woods, a second red fox scampered out. The hounds set out after him full tilt. We galloped on after them. Scent was obviously getting better. Though the hounds were at fault at times and needed to be recast under the expert guidance of Gerald, they could now run this fox. We followed, alternatively trotting, cantering, galloping, pausing or jumping. For half an hour, we ran briskly through the woods and up and down the hills. The going was superb; there was no frozen ground or snow, there was only a little bit of crackly ice as we splashed across rocky stream beds. Because we were hunting in the Cheshire Saturday country, there were many stout fences to be jumped, including chicken coops, stake-and-bounds (pickets stacked one on top of another and bound together), three-rail line fences and panels of three phone poles stacked one on top of another. Thoughts of all else melted away in the excitement of riding all out as I strove to control Peter and set him carefully for each jump. In between these brisk gallops, at a check the field chatted easily with one another. After all, many of us had been hunting together for years. Some members hunted two or even three days a week, though others, like me, could only get out on Saturdays. In addition, many of the field saw one another repeatedly in and around Unionville between hunting days.

Finally, the second fox went to earth. At 2:30 or so, Peter was beginning to get just a tad tired. As we pounded up one of the mile-long hills, he huffed heavily. As we crossed plowed fields, I could feel his energy draining out of his big body. After all, he weighed 1,700 pounds himself (not considering the 203 pounds of my dead weight, plus my boots, a heavy hunting saddle and other tack). In jumping over a fence, Peter had to overcome the force of gravity which is always trying to bring a horse and rider down to earth and is always ready to embrace the rider if, in fact, the rider should come unglued going over a fence. (I was to prove that again a couple of times later that very afternoon.) By 2:30, we had already had a good day, hunting seven or eight miles, jumping twenty or so good fences, and galloping up and down the beautiful grassy hills west of Unionville.

There was a check on top of a high hill just west of the Cheshire Kennels. The hounds were sniffing around a collection of huge rolled up hay bales. They then went down into the valley. Peter the Great and I were standing at some little distance from the rest of the field. I took my feet out of my handsome Tibetan stirrups and stretched my legs and knees. I looked westward down the hill and across the stream and the broad valley and then westward all the way to Coatesville and indeed well beyond. The placid well watered and wooded countryside and the intervening fields stretched out in front of me. The winter sun warmed my back. All my problems and vexations had somehow seemed to have grown smaller. How lucky I was to be able to enjoy the countryside, my horse, the sport and the company!

I could see Mrs. Hannum's blue Jeep bumping roughly up and down across the plowed field on the other side of the valley. As always, she was doing everything she could to help the hunt. Once again, I was most grateful for her care and affection for the sport and for those lucky ones, like me, for whom she laid it on. My happy meditations were quite suddenly interrupted by the Huntsman's horn. The hounds had found a third fox. By now, scent, that magical elixir to the hounds' sensitive noses, had become excellent. They were now running wide open, catching the scent breast high. We jumped a chicken coop and followed the hounds into the woods and up to the top of the hill. The hounds went left handed. We fairly flew out of the woods and then came pounding down a long hill. At the bottom, there was a three-rail fence. I knew from former hunts that there was a strand of tightly strung barbed wire just below the top fence rail to keep the cattle in since the fence itself was somewhat ancient and rotten. It was important to keep this strand of wire in mind since, if the top rail were busted out, the next horse and rider might go to the panel where the top rail was knocked out in order to save a tired horse from a three-rail jump. However if one hit the almost invisible strand of silvery barbed wire, there could be most unpleasant consequences for horse and rider. Fortunately, the whole field jumped the fence cleanly. No rails were broken.

Peter sized the situation up carefully and jumped on over in a giant, but delicate, bound. On the far side there was a bank, then a cinder road. Beyond the road was another three-rail fence and then a muddy bog. The Field Master and the first flight jumped the fence on the far side of the road. But, after the first jump, I pulled Peter sharply to the left and galloped on down the cinder road. I then jumped into the field at an inset panel beyond the bog, and I came charging on up the long hill. The rest of the field had followed along on behind the Field Master through the soft muddy bog. I met the rest of the field near the top of the hill. We all galloped together towards another three-railer right at the very top of the hill and sailed on over.

Ahead came the happy sounds of hounds in full cry and Gerald's horn blowing the notes of "Gone Away" to encourage the fox, horses, hounds and riders. There was a momentary check. Then hounds were away once again. We continued on across the top of the hill towards a fence that last year had unseated me on almost the first day of the season. I pointed Peter carefully towards the fence, encouraged him with a nudge of my unspurred boots. Peter carefully stood back and fairly sailed over the fence. However, a fellow foxhunter was not as fortunate: there he was on one side of the fence with his horse galloping madly away one the other, bridle and irons flapping. Another member of the field caught the horse's bridle. Mercifully, the rider had not been hurt.

We continued and then turned right and jumped into a big field that lies directly west of the kennels. After another check and a view, we came barreling over a fence and to a field full of cattle. One of the young heifers playfully chased the whip, Larry Snyder, down to the bottom of the hill, distracting him from his serious work. Our fox was now in the kennel woods. Quite suddenly, the fox snuck out to the right at the very corner of these woods, loping easily and confidently along with an occasional backward glance. He first went right but then veered sharply left. The fox had been turned by riders coming up in front of him. His course was now directly across the lawn in front of the kennels. We galloped down the long hill and came up the other side.

The stiff three-rail kennel fence was outlined against the late afternoon wintery sky on top of the hill. This solid fence posed a real obstacle to our tired horses. The hunting staff had jumped safely, closely followed by the Field Master and most of the first flight. The remainder of the field was strung out all across the pasture so as to come at this big fence at right angles, picking a panel to try to jump this tough obstacle. A couple of tired horses flatly refused: they had had quite enough. Some of the riders prudently pulled up and called it a day. Others whose horses had refused, determined not to be left behind, circled their horses and gave their reluctant steeds a solid whack or two with a crop or hunting whip and a cluck or word of encouragement. Some of the horses, thus encouraged, went on over but others stuck to their tired guns and stayed on the near side of the fence. A few of the horses put in a small, close jump and somehow crawled over. Others were not so fortunate. The horse of a stablemate of mine slammed hard into the fence and the rider came off. As I came up the hill, the rider was up and obviously not hurt. But, he had his bridle in his hands. He waved me away from the broken panel because there was a silvery strand of barbed wire still tightly strung in place of the now broken rail. I veered around to the right, steadied Peter and put him at right angles to what seemed to be one of the lowest of the three-rail panels. At the last minute, Peter seemed to hesitate. Nevertheless, he did manage to jump cleanly on over the fence. Relieved, I galloped on across the lawn. The rest of the field was just sailing over an equally stout fence on the far side of the lawn. I steadied Peter and then clucked to him as I aimed him at this fence. Peter galloped full speed across the kennel lawn. I had my reins crossed and was seated well forward, fully expecting Peter to sail on over. At the very last minute, Peter slammed on his brakes and stopped dead. I catapulted over his head and the fence. I landed on my head and shoulder on the far side and rolled over.

My caliente helmet stood me in good stead: I was not hurt. After a moment, I got up. There was Peter looking somewhat surprised, standing on the other side of the fence. Fortunately, he had not run away as so many horses do when free of their rider. I was about to let out a volley of curses directed at Peter. When Mrs. Hannum's blue Jeep drew smartly up and stopped. She jumped efficiently out and grabbed Peter's bridle inquiring, "Is Peter all right?"

I replied somewhat drily, "Peter is okay, thanks, and so am I." I climbed back over the fence. Mrs. Hannum's passenger, Ramsay Buchan, often a whip, had also gotten out of the Jeep as had Mrs. Hannum's Jack Russell who was barking furiously with great excitement. Following Mrs. Hannum's brisk directions, Ramsay rolled down the tailgate of the Jeep. I clambered up. As Mrs. Hannum held Peter's bridle and Ramsay held my stirrup, I swung back aboard Peter. Mrs. Hannum pointed in the direction the hounds had gone. I set off after the hounds shouting, "Thanks for the help!" over my shoulder.

Galloping down the shoulder of Route 82, I came to a place where I could see the hounds and indeed the pink coats of the staff on a far hillside. A car follower opened a gate. We trotted gratefully on through. Then I gave Peter a gentle nudge with my heel and he galloped easily a mile or so across the top of the hills north of the kennels and caught up with the rest of the field where the hounds were momentarily in check. Then the fox was viewed again far off, still loping northward. We came to a small stake and bound fence. Would Peter jump? Urged on by a kick and a cluck, Peter tucked his feet neatly to the left and jumped handily over.

We were headed across the broad meadows north and east of the kennels towards a fence I had christened the "John McKenna Memorial Jump." Some three weeks before, John McKenna was riding his championship timber horse, Nick the Plumber, into this fence. Nick decided for some reason that this wasn't his day, or at least it wasn't his fence. Nick had jumped only halfway across the fence and had cut himself slightly on the barbed wire. Now, we were heading towards that fence again. Ahead of me, John McKenna was obviously taking care that this nemesis didn't halt him again. He had Nick the Plumber well in hand and gave him a couple of good belts with his riding crop. The horse got the message and jumped well and cleanly over the fence. Watching all this, I was confident that Peter would do likewise. I had my reins crossed and was sitting well forward as we pounded up to this fence. To my surprise, Peter stopped, slamming into the fence and cracking the top rail. Once again I rolled over his head and fell on the far side, cursing myself for my stupidity at not realizing that Peter had nothing left in him.

Nancy Miller came up, jumped down, and grabbed Peter's reins, who stood quietly enough. "Are you okay?" she asked, adding this advice: "Serious accidents happen when horses and riders get tired." Mrs. Hannum's blue Jeep came along: she again said, "Is Peter all right?" The tailgate was dropped again but, this time, Ramsay gave me a leg back up into the saddle. By the time all this was done, the staff and the field had disappeared from sight, still going northeasterly with hounds in full cry and the horn sounding faintly in the distance.

I followed Bruce Miller down around to the left of the tiny cover of pines where the fox had thrown the hounds off. Bruce, a Field Master for years, remarked "Eventually every fox will turn left or right. This fox will surely circle back to the place where he started from. Just stand here." Sure enough, we could hear the hounds in full cry in the distance but now coming back our way on a far hillside on the other side of Apple Road. The staff's horses' hooves clattered on the hard road below us as they pounded along, followed by the Field Master and one or two of the field, including Bruce Davidson's daughter, Nancy, Jeb Hannum and his English lady friend, Emily Debenham, all of whom had done a good job of keeping up with the hounds.

Quite suddenly, the hounds veered hard to the left and came up a small gully covered with weeds and second growth. The fox had jumped off the road and was ahead of the hounds in the thick underbrush choking the gully. The staff had to continue on the hard road: there was no place where they could get through the barbed wire and into that little gully and follow the hounds and, of course, the fox. As we stood there watching the hounds, Bruce Miller suddenly took off his caliente hat and pointed with it to the top of the hill: there was our hard pressed fox, now running hard with his tongue out. The hounds not more than 150 yards behind him in full cry. Bruce, his girls and the rest of the field galloped on around to catch up with the staff. I remained where I was and saw the fox go into a small thicket. The fox then came almost where he had gone in. The hounds were baffled: they did not want to run "heel" (running back in the direction the fox had come from).

After a full minute, the hounds figured out what the fox had done, found the correct line and were off again. I stood and watched for another moment. Then, I took a now slightly rested Peter and galloped him up to the top of the hill to the place where the fox had come out of the thicket. I stood "on the line" with my hat off, to mark the place for Gerald though the hounds had now gone on. The field and the staff came around the long way following at some distance behind the hounds. Peter and I were somewhat rested and not breathing so heavily, so we followed the field. We were coming to a telephone pole jump. After going down a steep hill and across the stream, I put Peter to the fence. Would he go over, or would he refuse? A good trooper, he galloped gallantly up to it, neatly tucked his feet to the left and sailed on over it and galloped away to the top of the next hill.

There was now another momentary check. Then the hounds were heard in the pine woods around to the right. We went down another hill with another telephone pole jump. Again, Peter carefully jumped over it and delicately threaded his way through the thick green pine woods with the rest of the field. By this time, the fox had swung right again. Clearly, he was going back towards the kennels and the safety of his den in that vicinity. We came to a fairly good sized panel that was inset into the field lying just east of the kennels. Again, my heart was in my mouth as I put Peter to it. Peter, by now, had recovered his stamina and will to jump. He jumped boldly over and then slithered down the steep bank, splashed across the icy stream and cantered up the other side.

The exultant baying of the pack of hounds in full cry abruptly stopped. The small residue of the field galloped up and found that our fox had had quite enough for that day: he had found his way to convenient earth and had gone down and in. That was the end of the hunt!

The hounds were gathered around the hole, sniffing, growling or pawing at it. Gerald jumped down from his lathered horse, throwing his reins to his whip, Larry, quietly congratulating each of his hounds, calling them in turn by name and giving them a congratulatory pat on the head. Then, pulling his horn out, he blew a long series of blasts on his horn right down the earthen hole, signaling to the fox, the hounds and the field that another hunting day was over.

The remaining members of the field stood about on their tired and lathered horses. There were only a few of the field there. Besides the staff, there were, of course, Bruce Davidson, the Field Master, and his wife, Carol, Nancy Davidson, Buzzy Hannum, Wendy Dixon, John McKenna, Stephanie Speakman, Bruce Miller and Blythe Miller and her friends, Jeb Hannum and Emily Debenham, Nancy Miller, Barbara Stewart and a few others. Peter, who had the habit of shaking himself like a Labrador dog after an icy swim, now indulged this quirk, shaking me from the top of my caliente hat covered with Unionville dirt right down to my muddy boots.

Mrs. Hannum bumped up saying, "I guess everyone agrees it's time to call it a day. But what a day! Well done one and all." It was well past 4:30. The wintery sun was going down and the temperature had fallen. Both horses and riders were dead tired. We had had a magnificent day, outstanding even among the many glorious days that season. Gerald now sounded his horn again and again, summoning the hounds who had gotten lost or fallen behind. By one's and two's, they came out of the woods and corners of the fields, joining their fellows, being welcomed back with a growl or a sniff. When all of the hounds were accounted for, Gerald turned homeward.

I said, "Goodnight and thanks for all your help", to Mrs. Hannum.

She replied, "It really was a good day, wasn't it? You and Peter did well. I am glad you are both all right."

I rode over to Gerald and said, "Gerald, you and your hounds have done your-selves proud. That's a fact." I also thanked Larry and Monk.

Finally, I went over to Bruce Davidson, the Field Master, and said, "There were at least two especially big jumps that I shall never forget among the seventy or eighty that we followed you over today. Thanks for a glorious day of sport."

We ambled back towards the kennels recounting to one another the exciting phases of the hunt. Arch had brought Nancy Miller's van from the meeting place to the kennels so that we did not have to ride three or four additional miles on our tired horses. Arch, who had followed by car, shared the excitement of the riders as we dismounted on the kennel lawn, loosening girths, pulling stirrups up and throwing sheets and blankets across the sweaty horses. Arch passed out Tootsie Rolls and everyone downed them, ravenously hungry after more than five hours in the saddle. As the last horse went into the van, I wished everybody "goodnight." Still shaking our heads with pleasure and disbelief over what had been a superb day, especially since nobody had been hurt in the many, many spills, we each went our separate ways.

I was driven back to my car. Once at my car, I pulled off my muddy hunting coat and mud-covered caliente helmet and threw them in the trunk of my car. I wiped most of the splattered mud off my boots and pulled on my chino trousers, a rumpled sweater and the old sports coat and put a tweed cap on. I pulled away with a last wave. Then I ate the last Tootsie Roll. I wolfed down the stump of a loaf of homemade bread and the bit of Priscilla's Christmas ham. I washed the bread and ham down with great gulps from the blue Australian bottle of beer that I had providentially put in my hunting bag so many hours ago.

I turned the car around and drove eastward, savoring the day's sport. I was thank-ful that neither Peter nor I had not been hurt in our two towering falls and that we two had managed to be there among the field at the very end of this glorious day. All of my various problems had now been shrunk to Lilliputian size by hard exercise and excite-ment. I was comfortably tired. As I drove along, I heard on the radio the somber notes of the last act of *Don Carlos*.

I remembered that I had said I would stop in to see the Wyeths. I had the proposed contract from IBM in my briefcase, and I had promised to go over that with Betsy. More importantly, it was always fun to see them.

I telephoned Betsy. "Sure," she said, "come on along. I would be glad to go over the IBM matter. Andy will be along in an hour or so." I drove down Route 1 and turned left on Route 100 at Hank Smedley's diner just past the Brandywine River Museum and just below the Chadds Ford Inn where I had spent so many long evenings carousing with Jack and Eleanor Flaherty before the inn became a really fancy restaurant. I then went up winding Route 100 that circled through the marshes alongside the Brandywine until I came to the cluster of soft lights illuminating the Wyeth buildings, the Mill, the Ark and Andy and Betsy's house. I turned left down the graveled lane, past the evergreens now well above the grass that had replaced the picket fence which had offended the zoning laws of the Township so many years ago, past the standard where the alarm light lit up and on down onto the cobbles and past the straw beehive and up to the lean-to parking shed where I parked. I knocked: the top of the Dutch door swung open. There stood Betsy outlined against the light of the living room, momentarily reminding me of a painting that Andy had once done of her leaning on just such an open Dutch door. Nome, the white Samoyed dog with long snow protective eye lashes, wiggled all over with pleasure at seeing me (as she would indeed for anyone).

After exchanging greetings with my smiling black-haired hostess, I instinctively looked to the left where, the last time I had been to see Andy and Betsy, there had been the picture of a new Marconi-rigged schooner tied up in a secret cove. As I had tried to talk to Betsy I kept looking over her shoulder at a huge new picture, "Snow Hill," hanging there. In the center of a wintery snow-covered hill was an implausible maypole with a tiny Christmas tree at the very top. On either side were miniature replicas of some of the familiar houses and farms that had appeared in Andy's work over the last fifty years. With their backs "to the camera," there were dancing, frolicsome figures of most of Andy's portrait figures. Among others, I recognized Otto in his helmet and a long gray German Army coat, there was Helga with her pigtail, there was the black man, and others. They were all dancing around this wintery maypole in the snow. I was staggered by this retrospective picture.

My replies to Betsy's questions and inquiries on other matters were incoherent as I looked back again and again at this newest picture. Obviously, Betsy was pleased that I liked this joyous but enigmatic picture: it summed up a whole lifetime of life and work as well as many other things. I said, "Don't allow any copies to be made of this picture, retain it forever. I am sure that the critics will carp, as always, but everyone in their right mind will like it."

After I had drunk my fill of this picture, we sat down at the long polished oat table with the heavy silver tankards on it. I smoked a proffered cigarette (though I had not had one since my birthday). I knew that I had better discuss the IBM computer contract with Betsy before Andy came in since that clearly was not his "dish of tea." We spent an hour going over the contract. When we were done, Betsy said, "Andy should be here any time now, and Jamie is coming for dinner."

Just then, Nome barked at the sound of a car. The door banged open, and Andy came bustling in, in a large coyote coat. As usual on Saturdays, he had been working in his studio all day long. Clearly, he was ready to relax.

Andy looked at my muddy boots and said, "Well, I see that you've been out hunting foxes again. Did you catch any poor foxes?"

"No, Andy," I replied, "but we chased a number and sailed over any number of fences."

Andy said, "You know, I haven't done many horse pictures. But I did an early one of a white horse. It was stolen or somehow disappeared and it has never turned up again. Right, Betsy?"

Betsy replied, "That's right, but you did do an early watercolor of Gilbert Mather, the Master of the Brandywine Hounds, sitting on his horse on a hillside somewhere in Chester County. I don't know quite where it was."

Andy said, "In the picture, Mr. Mather has on a brown coat rather than a black or red coat. Do you know why? My father, N. C. Wyeth, knew Mr. Mather well. My father said that when Gilbert Mather formed the Brandywine Hounds in 1907, he went to his Quaker neighbors, who farmed the country over which he wanted to hunt. He asked for permission to hunt his hounds over their land. The reply was, 'Yes. Thee may hunt over our lands, Brother Mather, but we would prefer that thee not wear pink or scarlet coats.' Mr. Mather courteously said, 'I suppose the reason is that the sight of pink coats in your quiet countryside would offend Quaker sensibilities.' Their reply was, 'Not at all, Brother Mather. The fact of the matter is that the last time there were red coats seen in the Brandywine Valley, it was the British and the Hessian soldiers on their way to the Battle of the Brandywine.' My father said that Gilbert Mather was surprised but, of course, acceded to their request, remembering that, after all, it was only about three long generations back to the Battle of the Brandywine. Things die hard in the country."

I said, "I never knew that. I always sort of wondered why he was in a brown coat. I know the picture well. It hangs in the Christiana Room of the Hotel DuPont. It's a terrific picture of a Master on a cold wintery day: clearly, he has lost his hounds."

Andy said, "Did you know that General Washington displayed his great ability as a horseman and a foxhunter when he galloped cross country right back of here in the middle of the Battle of the Brandywine? He heard rifle fire around on his right. General Cornwall had sent the British army across the upper fords of the Brandywine to outflank Washington. Maxwell's corps held while Sullivan attempted to wheel the American right wing about. Washington, who had been 'entertained' at Chadds Ford by the Hessian General Kniphauser, galloped cross country, sailing over fences and leaving his staff and young aides behind him. When he got there, Washington helped rally the fleeing American right wing. Though Brandywine was a big defeat, it might have been a total disaster and perhaps the end of the Revolution except for Washington's cross country ride."

"I did know that from old Chris Ward's wonderful book, The *Wars of the Revolution*, but I had not realized the significance of Washington's wild cross country ride. But, incidentally, do you know that the British had their buglers play the foxhunting call 'Gone to Earth' at the Battle of Kipp's Bay when the American Rangers were retreating? But General Washington had his foxhunting revenge by having the tune 'It's a Fine Foxchase' played at the Battle of Princeton."

I added, "Andy, I really like your new picture."

Andy replied genially, "People are going to say 'Wyeth has now flipped his wig for sure. We knew all along it was coming, ever since he painted that dead man lying naked, half covered with snow in his coffin.' "

Still, I knew, as always, he was pleased and assured to hear that someone, anyone (even me) took pleasure in seeing his most recent work.

When I had been there a couple of weeks before, Andy and I had managed somehow, after a couple of belts of vodka, to exchange eyeglasses. I said to Andy as we exchanged back again, "If 'Snow Hill' is a result of changing glasses, I think it's all to the good."

Andy said, "I think the change was the result of vodka. Speaking of which, shall we?" He walked over to the counter and pulled out three tumblers, some ice and poured out vodka. Betsy took hers with tonic. We all sat back down at the long table. With Nome nuzzling each of us alternatively for attention, we "chewed the fat," including Tom Watson, President Bush, Colonel North, as well as local Delaware and Pennsylvania people. The new book on Andy which Richard Meryman was writing came up. Andy said, "God knows I want the truth, but sort of dread it."

At 6:30, Jamie walked in for dinner: he was a temporary bachelor since his wife, Phyllis, was off to see her mother, Mrs. James Mills, down in Virginia. We talked briefly about the Grand Opera House Gala held early in January to which Rudolph Nuryev had come with his troop of students and performed at Jamie's request. We also gossiped about this and that, including recent divorces and separations, and who had died around Wilmington. At 7:00, I firmly declined a third drink and said good-bye. I said, "I am off to see *Dangerous Liaisons* at the Tri-State Mall at the foot of Naaman's Road. I am told that it is visually as impressive as *Barry Lyndon*, musically as impressive as *Amadeus*, and as much fun as *Tom Jones*."

With the week's activities, the day's fox hunting and the heavy hand of my host, I wondered as I drove off whether it was really prudent for me to drive. I also thought I would probably sleep through the movie. However, I found my way safely down to the bottom of Naaman's Road. When I got into the mall area close to the theater, I was assailed with the smell of stale popcorn. I was afraid that I might not be able to get a ticket. However, there were only ten or so people waiting in line for tickets and probably only sixty or so in line for the quad of theaters. When I got to the head of the line, I saw that Senior Citizens were entitled to a $2 reduction. I paused for a moment before deciding to admit that I was a "Senior Citizen" by tendering the reduced ticket price. In the end, my Scotch-Irish frugality prevailed: Thus, I ponied up only $3.

The young high school girl serving as cashier said "But the price of a ticket is $5."

I said with a smirk, "But I am a Senior Citizen."

She looked back at me and (God bless her) said, "I almost don't believe you." I could have squeezed her little hand for that somewhat backhanded compliment. Her little finger punched the ticket machine and it plunked out a ticket. She took my $3.

I walked on back to the line for the 7:30 movie pleased as punch. I then spied a pet shop and thought that I would zip in and get Annie a tropical fish of some kind for her Christmas aquarium. I picked out a 3-inch miniature sand shark. I was about to buy it when the short, stout lady in charge of the shop said, "Mister, that shark won't last through any movie."

I said, "Well, I will come back afterwards and buy it."

She said with finality, "I sure as hell am not going to stay open that late to sell one itty-bitty shark." I found my way back into the line which had now grown larger. I strolled on into the theater. The movie started right on time.

My fears of going to sleep were swept away from the moment the classical French figures came on the screen and the evil, twisted plot of *Dangerous Liaisons* began to unfold. Glen Close was marvelous. The man who played the male lead was not really convincing but the rest of the characters were fabulous as was the decor and the music. I was fascinated as I watched this tale of hatred, greed and sensuality unfold. As it swept to a dramatic and sad climax, my Presbyterian view that evil was its own reward was reconfirmed.

At 10:30 or so, the movie was over. I hurried on out but the fish store was tightly buttoned up: no shark for Annie. I was once again in the sordid world of the Tri-State Mall with fumes of popcorn all around me. I retrieved my car and headed toward New Castle. I swept along at 70 miles an hour down by the Delaware River with the lights of Wilmington, this time on my right and the river with the twinkling lights of the New Jersey shore on my left. I went a mile or so further into the eastern end of New Castle. The lighted steeple of Immanuel Church rose over the peaceful Colonial town of New Castle. It provided a homing beacon in more ways than one. I parked my car in front of 53 The Strand and came on in.

I carried all my accumulated stuff in and sorted it out—dirty laundry in the wash basket for Marie, my housekeeper, dirty shirts for the laundry. I washed my boots and brushed my mud-splattered coat. I brushed my teeth and took two Tylenol. At 11:30, I jumped into my bed. I read a few pages of Joyce, then turned the light out as the biggest bell in the Immanuel belfry solemnly sounded twelve times. I looked out the window: way out across the Delaware River a ghostly container ship was swiftly and silently standing downriver in the darkness. I went lightly to sleep. Hunting had done its work.

BATH COUNTY

In Xanadu did Kubla Khan a stately pleasure dome decree . . .
COLERIDGE

Miss Anne DeB. Prickett
Smith College
Northampton, MA

Dear Annie,

As you know, George Ohrstrom invited both of us to Bath County, Virginia, to hunt with the Bath County Hounds over the Labor Day Weekend. I had hoped that this could be your first fox hunt. However, that was impossible because you and Charlie, your horse, needed to be in Northhampton, Massachusetts to start your second year at Smith. It is going to be a challenging year for you, especially since you have signed up for a heavy pre-veterinary schedule.

Actually, the genesis of this hunting trip all started quite some time ago when Peter Winants told me how much he had been enjoying hunting in the late summer and early fall in Bath County, Virginia. He said that our friend, George Ohrstrom, who had had to give up hunting himself after years as an active foxhunter and president of the Orange County Hounds in Middleburg, had decided to reestablish this small hunt in Bath County about seven years ago. "The Bath County Hounds," Peter said, "is ideal for those who have learned that foxhunting is far more than the 'run and jump' hunting that I have done for so many years." I also had gradually come to the theoretical realization that fox-hunting does involve great skill, knowledge and concentration by the Master of the Foxhounds, the Huntsman and his whips as well as the Field Master. But, when it came to actual hunting, not only am I usually fully preoccupied with my horse but also I am usually not in a position to see, much less understand, what the Huntsman and his

Melvin Poe. Photographer: Janet Hitchens, Middleburg, Virginia.

hounds are really up to.

I talked further with Peter about Bath County and asked him why Bath County is such fine hunting.

Peter replied, "Why, because it's really beautiful country. There is none of the urban sprawl or development that crowds and interferes with most hunts today. Bath County must be still like it was when young George Washington came up from Tidewater, Virginia, to survey the country before his participation in General Braddack's ill-fated campaign in the 1750s. There is no jumping since the big fields and pastures lying in the valley alongside the Jackson River have all been gated with latches that can be easily opened from horse-back. The gates themselves are so evenly balanced that they swing open and stay open until they are pushed closed and then latch themselves. The real reason that Bath County is so good for hunting is everyone gets to hunt right up with Melvin Poe, the legendary Huntsman who, for about twenty-five years, was the Huntsman for the Old Dominion Hunt and then hunted the hounds for another twenty-five years or so with Orange County.

"George was able to prevail on Melvin when he retired from hunting the Orange County Hounds to come down on hunting days and/or weekends to Bath County to hunt, bringing with him 12 to 14 couples of senior Orange County hounds. Melvin hunts these familiar and veteran hounds without a large field pressing him, the hounds and the fox too closely. Come try it. You'll love it."

When George heard from Peter that I was interested in hunting in Bath County, he

Melvin Poe. Photographer: Janet Hitchens, Middleburg, Virginia.

promptly telephoned me and invited me to come down. Annie, when George heard that you are a rider, he included you. I then received a mimeographed Bath County fixture card for the fall of 1996. Scrawled at the top was a note from Peter saying, "Bill, get back to me with the best date for you."

I immediately telephoned Peter: we agreed on the Labor Day Weekend. Peter later told me that George decided that he himself would come down to act personally as our host and guide, saying he would enjoy vicariously the sport with us and through us.

I therefore got up on the Saturday of the Labor Day Weekend and said good-bye to Caroline. She wholeheartedly gave me her blessing and best wishes for good hunting. I drove my Blazer with a borrowed trailer up to Nancy Miller's stable outside of Unionville. My saddle, bridle and cooler were loaded in the back of my Blazer. Nancy led Babar right into the trailer and I snapped the nylon webbing behind him. Nancy and I heaved the heavy trailer ramp up together. I personally hand tightened the large butterfly nuts that secured the trailer ramp. With a wave to Nancy, I eased out of her drive and drove on down to I-95 and so on across the bridge over the Susquehanna.

I was rolling along down towards Washington, D.C., happily listening to the tape of Mozart's "Piano Concerto No. 24." A lady in a passing car wildly motioned to the back of the trailer. I looked in my mirror: to my horror, I could see that the trailer ramp had come down and was bumping and banging on the concrete road, causing a cascade of sparks. I cut Mr. Mozart off in mid-cadenza, pulled sharply onto the shoulder of I-95 and stopped. Mercifully, Babar had not panicked

Melvin Poe, Huntsman. Photographer: Janet Hitchens, Middleburg, Virginia.

or put his full weight against the webbing when the trailer door had flopped open and then banged and bounced along the highway. Instead, he was just nonchalantly leaning against the webbing and contentedly nibbling on the hay in his rope hay net. Shaken, I heaved the trailer ramp back up and tightened the big butterfly bolts down as hard as I could by hand and then got out my hammer and gave each butterfly nut ten hard whacks. I shuddered then (and shudder now) to think what would have happened if Babar had panicked or the nylon webbing had broken or given way causing Babar to exit backward onto I-95 as I was rolling along at 70 miles an hour!

I arrived at George's place in Middleburg at lunch time and was welcomed by my host, George, as well as Peter Winants. George introduced me to John Coles and his daughter, 12-year-old Fraley. John assured Peter and me that George's van could take John's horse and his wife Julie's horse as well as their children's three white ponies, and could also carry Babar and Peter's horse, Morsby. He said it was quite unnecessary for Peter and me to drive our trailers down to Bath County. The van left, driven by John, accompanied by Fraley. Julie Coles and the other two Coles children, Peyton and Sloane, were driving down later. We had lunch, loaded our stuff into George's Jeep Station Wagon, and we were off with Peter at the wheel.

We had a fairly long drive ahead of us down through the beautiful northern Virginia country. I asked George how he came to re-establish the Bath County Hunt. George told me that Bath County had plenty of foxes and lots of country and was an ideal

Bath County Hounds. Photographer: Unknown.

place for foxhunters to have the opportunity to see how an expert hunts foxes as opposed to just riding and jumping a hunting horse and being always in the midst or back of the field. George added, "Then, I found that Melvin Poe was about to retire. I persuaded Melvin and his wife, Peggy, who had whipped some for her husband, to come on down from Hume, Virginia, where they live, to Bath County on hunting days. At the same time, we were able to get about twelve couples of Orange County hounds who were being replaced by young entry. John Coles who had worked with me for years agreed to handle the administration, and Peter was given the title and post of MFH. Peter's principal job has been to maintain good relations with our neighbors. Most of the farmers in Bath County are hound men or coon hunters. So, it's not too hard a job, is it, Peter?"

We drove on down through Virginia in a generally westward direction, going through small towns such as Buffalo Gap. We were in the hills and low mountains. Finally, we came up to Warm Spring Mountain. We stopped. There, stretched out below us, was the beautiful valley through which the Jackson River flows in a southeasterly direction in leisurely semicircles. On either side of the stream there were large hay fields and pastures. These fields ended where the wooded hills and low mountains rose out of the valley. The fullness of late summer was just beginning to give way to early fall. We came on down to the village of Warm Spring itself and passed by the circular public bath houses that had been built back in the 1750s or 1760s. Four or five miles further down the road we came to Fassifern, the original farm that George had purchased. A little distance off the main road we drove by George's three-and-a-half story wooden house. It had been an inn back in the colonial days. There was a kennel near the house where the hounds were kept on hunting weekends. Adjoining the inn was a two-story stone spring house, the bottom floor of which had served as a dank jail while the jailer and his family lived and slept in dry comfort up on the second floor.

We continued on down the dirt road that ran alongside the Jackson River flowing through the bottom of the valley. Eventually, we came in sight of a large white barn with a silo way down the valley. We rumbled across a pair of cattle guards. The van was parked at the barn. Babar, Morsby and the other horses had been unloaded and all were comfortably stabled in commodious box stalls with hay and water. We unloaded our saddles and tack. George decided that fording the Jackson River was the shortest way up to the guest house. So we splashed on across the river, up the muddy bank and through a gate and so to the guest house.

In the shank of the afternoon, we had a cold beer on the porch and looked down the long peaceful valley which we would hunt early the next morning. Peter had told me that once one came down into the valley, time stood still. Indeed, it did. The busy press and the frantic pace that all three of us normally followed was now totally behind us. We savored the late afternoon sunlight for an hour or so, talking about old times, old friends and, of course, foxhunting over the years. We then got back in the Jeep and drove back over to the old inn. The three of us came up the steps to the wide comfortable porch. Melvin Poe and his wife, Peggy, were there with their daughter, Patty, and her husband and a very cute red-headed grandchild. John and Julie Coles were there with their well mannered children, Peyton, Fraley, and Sloane. I was introduced all the way around, but

Melvin Poe, Huntsman. Photographer: Janet Hitchens, Middleburg, Virginia.

all the others knew each other well from having hunted together at Bath County. George went into the living room and caught up with everyone while Peter, John and I sat out on the porch with Melvin. Melvin, John and Peter kidded one another about the sweet white wine which Melvin made from wild grapes and dispensed to his guests, though he himself stuck to Coke. I sat there as the sun was getting ready to go down, smelling the delicious home cooked dinner on the stove while enjoying the sweet white wine. Peter asked, "Well, Melvin, just what sort of hunting are you going to show us tomorrow?"

Melvin said, "We'll go out kinda early, round about 7:00 o'clock 'cuz later in the day it gets sort of hot this time of year. The foxes are apt to lie up in their cool dens in the heat of the day. Also, scent isn't too good once the sun gets really up. However, as long as there is still some dew and fog in these valleys and also in the woods in the hills, you can do all right."

"I figure we'll set out and make a big clockwise circle looking to see if there are any foxes still around that have been out prowling and hunting during the night. After we have searched the covers down in the valley, we'll probably go up in the hills that you can see off there to the east and south. We'll be hunting up wind unless there is a change in the direction of the breeze that usually springs up around sunrise. Then we'll come back down from the hills and sweep the side of the valley that lies on this side of Jackson Creek. Though no one can guarantee anything so far as foxes are concerned, there sure are plenty of foxes around here. Some of them are bound to be out tomorrow morning. Of course, we have far too many deer in this valley as everyone does these days, but these Orange County hounds are deer proof. They wouldn't look up even if they were to go through a whole herd of deer. We also have some bears up in these hills, but, as you know, the hounds won't go after them either. They are pretty much foxhounds, and they stick to their business. We'll just go out and see what happens, shall we?"

Supper was announced. We all went in and sat at one long table feasting on delicious country ham, baked stuffed potatoes, golden yellow yams, biscuits, succotash, macaroni salad, local tomatoes followed by a huge pie with five sections, each of which was made with a different fruit (peach, apple, cherry, blackberry and raspberry). There was iced tea and good strong coffee as well as decaf.

After dinner, the three of us said good night all the way around. As we walked down from the porch, the moon had come up over the eastern hills and was lighting up this peaceful valley. Way down the valley, a cow or a steer was lowing. There was the bark of a house dog from a long way off. Below us could be hear the quiet gurgle of the Jackson River but, otherwise, it was all very still and placid.

Later, as I stood out on the porch of the guest house drinking in a last night view of the valley, I thought I heard in the far distance the high-pitched bark of a fox. (Perhaps the wish was father to the thought.) An owl was hooting eerily in the woods nearby.

On Sunday, we were up early. It was a cool and beautiful morning. Every blade of grass twinkled with dew in the early sunlight. Peter and I got dressed in informal hunting clothes—boots, breeches, short sleeve shirts and caliente hats. After a modest breakfast, George drove us over to the stable. Here, there was a welter of activity. Besides Melvin and his daughter, Patty, who were already on their horses, there were the three Coles children who, under the supervision of their father, John, and mother, Julie, curried their white ponies and saddled and bridled them up. John, Julie, Peter and I led our horses out and saddled and bridled them. Melvin was dressed in black boots, white breeches, a fireman's red shirt with red suspenders and a hunting cap (of course, with the ribbons down). When we were all mounted, the hounds were let out of the hound truck by Melvin's wife, Peggy. These were good big hounds, orange and white in color. The hounds obediently packed up behind Melvin who set out easterly towards the Jackson River. I remarked to Peter that Melvin didn't seem to have a horn. Peter replied that, of course, Melvin had a horn, but he only used it when he wanted to call the hounds back to him or sound an occasional advanced warning to the foxes. Otherwise, he controlled his hounds entirely by his voice calls. The two older Coles children, Peyton and Fraley, were appointed by Melvin to act as his whips. (The children did not carry whips.) Following Melvin's directions, they rode out on either side and slightly ahead of him, acting as his eyes and ears. The hunting was very relaxed with virtually no horn calls, no cracking of whips and only the Huntsman's soft calls now and again to the orange and white hounds. At the beginning, George followed us on the road in his Jeep.

After we splashed across the Jackson River, Melvin cast his hounds into a small cover on the far side. Melvin told us he was doing this because, though the cast was slightly down wind, he had seen three crows flying and wheeling all about there at sun-up. These birds might well have been fussing at a fox. But Melvin's first cast produced nothing. The hounds then hunted in and out for a quarter of an hour in an easterly direction under Melvin's watchful eye. None of the hounds opened. We then crossed a broad meadow after going through a gate which the youngest Coles, Sloane, nicely unlatched and closed behind us.

On the far side, Melvin again cast his hounds into the woods that stretched along the lower part of the hills. The orange-colored hounds could be seen working in and out of the trees and undergrowth. Finally, one hound opened hesitantly. We broke into a slow lope and followed Melvin over in the general direction where the hound had opened. The other hounds had stopped and looked up expectantly and then had also gone in the direction where their brother had opened. When they got in his vicinity, some hounds also opened but somewhat dubiously. Melvin encouraged his hounds with voice calls to them. Like all Huntsmen, the words he used in "talking" to the hounds were unintelligible, at least to me. The scent was obviously elusive: the hounds first found and then lost the scent. When they were at fault, the pack was cast by Melvin in ever widening circles until they picked the scent up again. They hunted this way in start-and-stop fashion for a half a mile or so with Melvin gently encouraging them as they went along and coaching them when they were at fault. Finally, the scent just plain petered out. John told me this was undoubtedly a fox who had been this way hours before, perhaps even during the night. The hounds had been tracking him by what little was left of the scent.

We then followed Melvin and his two young whips up and up into the hills standing in our stirrups and holding on our horses' martingales or their manes. At the top, the hounds opened again, going straight down the steep hill. We turned and followed Melvin back down to the floor of the valley, leaning way back in our saddles, bracing ourselves with our feet in the stirrups. The hounds were still not running flat out but instead were carefully hunting along on what was obviously another old line. They hunted through three big fields. We kept rising and standing in our stirrups looking far ahead, hoping to catch a view of the fox who had laid this scent down, but we never did catch sight of that fox.

The fox then turned leftward and went back up into the hills. Melvin followed his hounds on up again and we came after him. Eventually, we found the hounds all clustered around a small hole in a bank with fresh earth that had been thrown out of the hole. Melvin pulled his horn out of his pocket and blew "Gone to Earth." He said, "Boys and Girls, the scent isn't very good today. But, in spite of poor scent, it seems to me the hounds have done a right good job in following this old fox down into the valley, back up again and putting him right smack dab into his den."

Melvin turned his horse around and called to his hounds by name. The hounds stopped circling around and trying to burrow down the hole and fell in behind him. Melvin led us back down again to the floor of the valley and then turned northward. Melvin said that he was going to sweep a small bit of woods where he had often found a fox. He brought his pack of hounds carefully around to the up wind edge of this covert. With a gesture of his arm, he freed them, so to speak, and sent them on in to the covert, giving a toot or two on his horn as a warning to any fox who might be dozing in the midmorning warmth of the late summer sun. However, his warning fell on deaf ears, so to speak, because when the hounds came out the other side, the covert was bare.

We then splashed across the shallow slow moving Jackson River and went up on the other side toward the hills on the north side. We passed a small patch of sweet corn, all trampled and smashed down. Patty asked her father, "Dad, what in the world got into that corn?"

Melvin replied as we rode by this scene of maize havoc, "A black bear did that. They go crazy when they get loose in a field of sweet corn. The poor farmer won't get anything at all out of his corn patch."

We then turned eastward again and could see Fassifern's roof and chimneys some four miles up the valley. By now, the sun was high overhead and the dew had all evaporated. It was getting hot. We walked along or trotted behind Melvin and the hounds. I thought surely we would find nothing more that morning, but Melvin and his hounds proved me wrong.

As we came down a broad grassy slope, suddenly there was a tally ho from Peyton. Ahead and to Melvin's right, there was a flash of red with a spot of white on its flowing tail: it was a small red fox running swiftly eastward. At first, the hounds did not see or scent the fox, but Melvin quickly lifted them and put them on the line. When they picked up the line, the hounds took off, making a great sound that reverberated up and down the valley.

Sloane said as she cantered along, "Mom, I hope the fox gets away."

Julie replied, "Not to worry, dear, he will!" Scent was plainly non-existent. When we had started this fox, we were fairly close to it. But the hounds had to be cast and recast by Melvin. Finally, it was clear that our little fox had either eluded the hounds or had simply run fast enough and far enough so that we lost him.

We now fetched up at a fence with a gate through it. Julie Coles cautioned her children and indeed all of us not to go through the gate. Not fifteen feet on the other side, she warned us there was a steep hill that went down almost perpendicularly 200 feet.

As we stood there, Melvin said, "I don't think we can do no better today. Agreed we call it a day?"

The horn was brought out, Laggard orange and white hounds came on in, by ones and twos, wagging their sterns. Eventually, the hounds were all accounted for. Peggy drove the hound truck up, the back door was opened and the hounds jumped in. Melvin got off his horse and rode on back to Fassifern in the hound truck while his daughter, Patty, ponied his horse on home.

We had about three miles or so back to the white barn. We ambled down the long hills and through the grassy pastures, crossing and recrossing the Jackson River a couple of times. The Coles children skylarked a bit on their ponies. We got back to the stable and dismounted. The horses and ponies were all hosed down and scraped off and put away in the barn.

We went back up to the old inn and had a huge "breakfast" consisting of ham and eggs, toast, grits, biscuits, bacon, tomatoes, macaroni casserole, pie, coffee and ice tea and soda for the children. While this was being put on the table, Peter, John and I again sat out on the porch with Melvin for another taste of his sweet white wine.

Melvin said, "All in all, considering the poor scenting, it was a good day of hunting. My hounds worked well. We made the most of today, accounting for one fox and chasing a couple of others." We agreed with him.

Afterwards, good-byes were said all the way around. All the horses and ponies were loaded in the big van. George and Peter slept as I drove the Jeep back up to Middleburg. There, Babar was unloaded from the big horse van and put in my borrowed trailer. Everyone had a hand in tightening and checking the butterfly nuts.

After saying good-bye and thanks to George and Peter for the wonderful hunting with the Bath County Hounds, I got on the road homeward. I realized that I had finally seen what foxhunting is truly about. It was not just the run and jump excitement I had enjoyed so much over all these years. It was all of that and much, much more. Rather, the core of foxhunting lay in watching the careful and meticulous skill of the Huntsman and his whips and hounds versus the guile of the fox. I had been missing the forest for the trees. Clearly, there had to be a lot more to foxhunting than I had been seeing. Now, at long last, I had seen the light. Rowe used to say, "Better late than never."

As I drove northward, I also thought about the fact that once again I had been the recipient of the generosity of yet another person who had created a wonderful foxhunting opportunity for me and others. This time, it was George Ohrstrom who had developed and supported the Bath County Hounds though he himself could no longer actively foxhunt. It had been a real eye-opener into the real meaning of foxhunting. As I thought about this, I wondered how I could somehow repay what I owed to all those who had made foxhunting possible for me.

George L. Ohrstrom, Jr.
Photographer: Unknown.

I had learned something else. When I stopped to get gas, you can bet I rechecked all the butterfly nuts! Rowe used to say, "Some people get older and wiser: don't be one of the ones who just get older."

When I got back to Unionville, Nancy was waiting. At her urging, I told her all about the quiet wonders of Bath County hunting. She said, "Well, I am glad you had such a fine time and learned something about foxhunting. I am also glad you and good old Babar are both back safe and sound." Only then did I tell her about the potentially disastrous mishap with the trailer ramp. Nancy blanched visibly, saying, "Oh my God!" She went right over to Babar's stall and patted him as if to assure herself that Elephant Man, as she called him, had not fallen out but was really okay.

This, then, Annie, is my account of the Bath County Hunt. After all these years, I still have not had a chance to show you what a pleasure foxhunting is. I do hope that in years to come you and I will be asked down to Bath County by George and that you will be able to come so we can enjoy foxhunting together behind Melvin and his orange colored hounds in that beautiful valley.

Affectionately,

Your Dad

THE APRICOT FOX

"All's well that ends well!"
SHAKESPEARE

Babar, my faithful hunting horse, had had "front end" problems for a couple of years—that is, he went lame time and time again in his right front foot and leg.

One old farrier said "Shucks, I don't understand for the life of me how Babar stands up much less how he goes on galloping and jumping." Neither Nancy Miller's kindly ministrations nor all the veterinarians round about nor even the prestigious University of Pennsylvania Veterinary Center at New Bolton could find out exactly what was the matter, much less find a cure for Babar. At one point they even "nuked" Babar in the nuclear laboratory. In the fall of 1996, Nancy brought him in after a summer of rest in good green pastures. Nothing seemed to be able to get Babar to come sound.

One day, she said sadly of Babar, or Elephant Man, as she called him, "I am at the end of my rope with dear old Elephant Man. There is no solution but to find you a new hunting horse."

That presented a major problem. I not only needed a horse who could carry my ever increasing weight but one who could jump the big Unionville fences without any real help or guidance from me. On the other hand, I had had another bad experience when I bought a flashy gray horse called Absolut. (Absolut was absolutely too much horse for me, but he has suited Wendy Dixon to a tee.) Again, Nancy mounted a search that extended from South Carolina to Maine. Finally she came up with a big bay gelding that she tried out for me and liked. Nancy thought Liberty would suit me and that I could handle him. Nancy hunted Liberty herself. In fact, she rode him on a day when Mrs. Hannum had designated her as the Field Master: Liberty had done well. Liberty turned out to be a big handsome cold blood (not a thoroughbred) horse, twelve or so years old. The lady owner was selling Liberty because she was having a hip replacement. I tried Liberty cross

Joe Cassidy, Huntsman, Cheshire Hunt. Photographer: James Graham, Montchanin, Delaware.

country somewhat gingerly before the winter closed foxhunting, and indeed all riding, completely down.

Though I had not actually hunted Liberty, at my wife Caroline's urging and indeed insistence, I bought Liberty. Caroline, in fact, told me, "What are you waiting for. Sure Liberty is expensive, but you of all people need a good hunter."

After Christmas, everything turned sour so far as my foxhunting was concerned. Babar continued lame. Personally, I had a series of difficult legal matters that took all my time. But, in any case, the atrocious winter weather made hunting impossible. However, each hunting day I would hopefully call the kennels at about 6:30 a.m. I always found Mrs. Hannum there. I would timidly ask, "Mrs. Hannum, is there any chance the hounds will go out today?"

She would sadly reply, "No, Bill. Unfortunately, there is just no possibility at all. There is just too much snow and ice." Or, alternatively, she would explain, "The pastures and fields of our neighbors are so soft and so full of water that we would endanger our permission to hunt across their property if we were to let the hunting field gallop across their sodden pastures. It would ruin their fields. Too bad. But, do please try again, won't you?"

I would try the next hunting day, and the day after that, only to find that due to the scourges of winter, foxhunting was just not possible. Week after week went by. There was

Nancy Hannum, MFH, Lawrence Snyder, Whip, Joe Cassidy, Huntsman of Cheshire Hounds. Photographer: James Graham, Montchanin, Delaware.

Joe Cassidy, Huntsman, Cheshire Hunt. Photographer: James Graham, Montchanin, Delaware.
Previous page: *Bruce Miller leading the field.*

no let-up in winter's grip. Nancy Miller said mournfully, "The only thing I and everyone else in Unionville can do is to exercise the hunters, including Liberty, by walking or trotting them up and down the hard roads."

But, finally, on a Thursday in March, quite out of the blue, so to speak, the weather suddenly broke and turned benign ("in like a lamb . . .") I called up the kennels. Mrs. Hannum, as always, answered. She said, her obvious pleasure spilling through the phone, "Oh, yes indeed, my yes, the hounds are going out today at 11 from Percy Pierce's gate. Bill, I certainly hope you can make it!"

I replied, "Indeed I will. See you there!" My hunting prayers had been answered.
I called Nancy Miller, "Have you heard the good news!"

She replied, "Yes, good news travel fast. See you at 10:45 where I usually park the van. We'll ride from there over to the meet."

Caroline, as I hung up the phone, said, "You don't have to say anything. I can tell from the smile on your face that hounds are going out. Good! I hope you have a wonderful day. Why don't you try Annie?"

My daughter, Annie, happened to be home from Smith College with her big Irish jumper, implausibly named Mountbatten but familiarly known as Charlie. Annie had been jumping Charlie with increasing courage, skill and determination in high jumping classes at horse shows for two years or so. But, she had never hunted, though I had repeatedly invited her to do from the time she first learned to jump when she was about eight.

However, Annie had quite recently remarked out of the blue quite off-handedly, "You know, Dad, Charlie hunted some with Cheshire before I bought him. he knows all about foxhunting. Some day he is going to take me foxhunting, just you wait and see!"

I telephoned Annie and woke her up. I said, "Annie, I know you don't think much of foxhunting but you've recently said you might try it some time, maybe just to please me. Well, how about today? Remember, Annie, we'll surely get more winter weather and foxhunting traditionally ends every year on St. Patrick's Day, March 17th."

To my great surprise and delight, Annie replied briskly, "Why, sure, I'd love to, Dad. That way, Charlie and I will have a chance to go out foxhunting with the Cheshire Hounds before we go back up to college tomorrow. Just where is the hunt meet and what time?"

I told Annie exactly where the meet was to be and how to get there and the time, "Remember, Annie, 11:00 a.m. sharp!"

Annie assured me, "Charlie and I will trailer to the meet on time. See you there, Dad."

Indeed, Annie was as good as her word. As I piled out of my car and stripped off my business suit and tied my stock, Annie was already up on Charlie. I was glad to see that Annie was correctly turned out and Charlie was well groomed. As soon as she saw me drive up, Nancy Miller, all smiles, had pulled Liberty out of her gooseneck trailer, stripped off his cooler and halter, retightened the girth and checked his tack all the way around. I climbed up on the tailgate of a pick-up truck. Nancy steadied Liberty with one hand and held my far stirrup as I got my left foot into the stirrup and swung heavily up and over and into the saddle. My artificial left knee audibly clicked. Liberty was plainly ready to go. I had to restrain him as Nancy swung lightly and gracefully aboard her own horse. Then, joining Annie and Charlie, we three ambled easily on down the road to Percy Pierce's gates.

Annie said, "Well, I for one am on the fox's side. I hope we do not catch a fox!"

I said, "Annie, we are all on the fox's side. No one wants to catch one or kill it."

Nancy said, "I hope the Apricot Fox we hunted all fall who dens down in this area is out today. He'll sure show us some sport!"

For a Thursday, there were a large number of foxhunters milling about, probably forty riders or so. Plainly, everyone was anxious to go out hunting again: it had been almost a full six weeks since the Cheshire hounds had been able to go out. Among those afoot was Vince Dugan helping to saddle up a pony for a small girl. When he saw Annie and me, Vince grinned and called out to me, "Well Dadeo, I see you are at long last going

Annie Prickett on Joyful; William Prickett on "Liberty". Photographer: Annie Jones, Unionville, Pennsylvania.

to get your wish. Good hunting to the pair of you."

Actually, just as we arrived, Joe Cassidy, the Huntsman, having been fully briefed by Mrs. Hannum and a plan for the day's hunting having been agreed upon, was about to blow his horn. As Mrs. Hannum herself was about to drive away in her old blue Jeep, I presented Annie to her. Mrs. Hannum, gracious as always, said, "You are welcome indeed, Annie. It's nice to see you finally out. We all know your father has been trying to get you to come out for years. I hope it will be a good day so that you will become a regular as your father is."

Joe Cassidy led his bitch pack through the brick gates followed by his whips, Larry Snyder, Oscar Crossan, and Anthony Jenks. Just behind them was Bruce Miller, the Field Master, that day, followed by the field. I introduced Annie to various foxhunter friends as we jogged along. Many already knew Annie and gave her a cheery welcome.

After Joe Cassidy hunted the pack carefully for about an hour without finding a fox, we came up to Annie Jones and my partner, Richie Jones. My goddaughter, Braxton, was beside them. When she saw my Annie alongside me, Annie Jones knew at once what a significant day this was for me and said, "Hi, Annie. How nice to see you out . . ."

Annie Jones suddenly stopped in mid-sentence. She was looking way across to the hill half a mile away. Then she stood straight up in her stirrups and boldly sang out, "Tally ho!" pointing to the hill. There indeed, halfway up on the far hillside calmly looking at us, was a beautiful fox sitting on his haunches, outlined against the bright green winter wheat.

Nancy Miller said, "By golly, that's the Apricot Fox all right. Get ready, we are in for a run!"

The fox himself languidly got up and loped easily up the hill, stopping twice to look over his shoulder at the hounds and foxhunters. There was a "Halloo" from Mrs. Hannum up the road far around to the left. There was a chorus of "Tally Hos" from the field and a volley of staccato notes from Joe's copper horn, blowing "Gone Away!" as Joe broke into a gallop to lead his hounds and the field to the hillside from which the fox was now quickly loping away.

The whole field also broke into a full gallop crossing the broad meadow toward a stout 3-rail line fence. Everyone was free to take their own line and pick their own panel of the fence. Liberty was pulling hard and going wide open, but, even so, Annie and Charlie galloped right on past us. I leaned back in my stirrups to check and rate Liberty somewhat as we came into this substantial jump. To the right and left of me, people were jumping up and over the fence. I saw Annie out of the corner of my right eye checking Charlie to allow a Cheshire regular to go roaring over the fence ahead of her: Annie and Charlie then sailed on over the fence. Liberty stood well back. I had anticipated a big jump from him so I was fully ready. He rewarded my confidence by flying cleanly over the fence. Liberty then galloped swiftly across the rest of the meadow and up the hill. Nancy pulled up alongside me, grinned and gave me a little thumbs up sign which I returned.

William Prickett on Libertyx. Photographer: Annie Jones, Unionville, Pennsylvania.
Next page: *William Prickett in the midst of Cheshire Field, Thanksgiving 1995.* Photographer: James Graham, Montchanin, Delaware.

By this time, the Apricot Fox and the hounds had gone on down the other side of the hill and into the woods. The hounds could be heard baying on ahead. The field, now bunched up, galloped en masse down the hill, into the woods, down through the deep rocky stream laced with gnarled roots and scrambled up the other side and then went full speed on up the hill through the woods and out over a chicken coop on the far side of the woods. Our fox then turned right. The hounds were still well ahead of us now running flat out in the fields below. Annie rode up to me as we checked, her young face and flushed with excitement. She pointed to our fox scampering swiftly along up to the top of the next hill and then disappearing over the crest of the hill.

We were led over a couple of stout jumps by the Field Master, Bruce Miller. Then, we came up on a small hill and went out over a telephone pole jump. We swung right handed and galloped through a pasture with turned-out horses who ran madly back and forth across our path toward a small three-rail fence, which we had to jump single file. We then went up to the corner of this field and went out over a large log, also single file. Annie was ahead of me and neatly jumped over the log jump, turned smartly left and disappeared around the corner. Liberty was hard to hold at the small checks and jumps since he was anxious to press forward. When we finally got a shot at the log jump, Liberty left me way behind and up in the air because he put in such a big jump. Fortunately, he was there below me when I came back down again. Thus, we galloped off together rather than separately.

Nancy came on by saying, "Are you okay?"

I shouted back, "Yep, I am still aboard Liberty, thank goodness!" and on we went.

Our path now lay through the woods and out into the fields east of the Wicks' house. We had another view of the Apricot Fox, now running flat out. The hounds appeared to be gaining on him. We then galloped towards Anne and Jock Hannum's house. The field was now all strung out. We put in a sharp left and went on down and out across the Newark Road and came up onto the Pennsylvania Hunt Cup course. There was a momentary check on the near side of a three-rail log fence. Liberty and I were panting heavily as were some others. Here, Liberty managed to inch his way up past Richie, Annie and Braxton Jones until he was right behind the Field Master, Bruce Miller. My Annie was right behind us.

Bruce looked behind him, saw us and said, "Annie, your father may not be the best turned out or the most knowledgeable or prettiest rider in the Unionville field, but he sure makes up for it by his enthusiasm."

Annie replied, "Well I guess that's sort of what counts."

Just then hounds opened ahead of us and Bruce put spurs to his horse and sailed on over the jump. Liberty was right behind him with Annie in my pocket (right on my heels). We barreled down the steep hill and flew on over a chicken coop as we came out of the woods. Hearing the hounds, Bruce led us left handed and came across the field in front of the Weymouths' house. We went over the line fence and on into the bog. After splashing along the muddy path through the bog, we jumped out the other side and then galloped flat out on across the broad field and then on over a pair of log jumps. Then we turned sharp right and came on up the road to the corner. The hounds were now well

Annie Prickett on "Charlie" and William Prickett on "Babar". Photographer: James Graham, Montchanin, Delaware.

ahead of us as we cantered up the shoulder of the road and jumped over a chicken coop and went into the woods under the power lines opposite the O'Brien house.

Mrs. Hannum was out of her blue Jeep saying a word of encouragement to each member of the field as they galloped on by. We turned right and came to a chicken coop: it had had a rider (a rail) across the top of it. Mercifully, one of the whips had pulled this rider since all the horses were now lathered and breathing heavily, especially since most of them had not been out in weeks except for road exercise. We jumped the coop and went around the pond and came on up towards the Del Basos' house.

At this point, our hard running fox was viewed again but clearly tired with his tongue hanging out. The hounds were briefly at fault. The hounds hunted through the marsh that runs up towards the Del Balso place. The Apricot Fox now came out of the top of the marsh. He was covered with mud. The hounds were on again and gaining on him, but the Apricot Fox went gamely on, running right by and deliberately disregarding a hole in the hillside at the top of the marsh.

Nancy exclaimed, "Darn! Why didn't he go into that hole?"

We jumped out on the road and galloped eastward alongside the road. At Newark Road, the hounds turned left handed and were going all out towards Mrs. Hannum's house, Broadlawn. Ahead of us, not 500 yards ahead of the hounds, we could see the Apricot Fox, now definitely moving ever more slowly.

Bruce Miller shouted, "The fox is making for his hole in the field opposite Broadlawn on the other side of the road."

But, it certainly looked to all of us like the Apricot Fox might not make it to the safety of his den. Annie, galloping alongside of me, cried out, "Dad! Dad! The hounds are gaining on that poor tired fox. They are going to catch him. Do something for gosh sakes, can't you!"

I shouted, as we galloped along, "Annie, what in the world can I do? I pray he will make it!"

But through my mind raced the grim words of Oscar Crossan some forty years ago when the Thanksgiving Fox had been turned. "There is almost no way a pack of hounds running hard on a line of good scent about to close in on a fox can be stopped."

Mrs. Hannum's blue Jeep appeared on the road we were riding toward, far around on our right and stopped. She jumped out and waved her arm. All of a sudden, the serious situation that we were galloping toward changed radically for the worse. Just then, to our left, moving slowly up the road toward us came a large yellow school bus. It drove right across the fox's intended course to his earth. To our horror, the fox was now forced to turn sharp, left. Instead of running across the road and to the safety of his hole, the fox was now running parallel to the road. The hounds also veered left and were now scarcely 200 yards behind him.

Joe, ahead of Bruce Miller, shouted to Bruce, "Bruce, hold the field!" Joe put spurs to his tired horse and gave a horn call to his three whips galloping far out to either side.

Bruce shouted to the field, "Hold hard—dammit—everyone hold hard right now! Hear me all you people!" As usual a couple of us were unable to pull up, so our horses galloped past Bruce.

He shouted angrily, "By God, I'll kill anyone who gets in the way of that fox!"

Everyone managed to pull up. The three whips came riding full speed in towards the pack, whirling their whips above their heads and cracking them and cracking them again. Joe galloped full speed through his pack and right up to the lead hounds. Joe was sounding "recall" on his horn and then started calling his lead hounds by name.

Some of the hounds finally began to raise their heads and left off running and baying. He pulled his horse up so sharply to a stop that the horse went back on his haunches. Joe swung down out of his saddle and jumped down right in front of his excited hounds. Joe threw his reins to his whip, Larry Snyder, who had galloped up. By then, all the hounds had raised their heads and stopped baying.

The Apricot Fox, now not a hundred yards ahead, also stopped for an instant, looked over his shoulder and then turned sharp right and ran on across the road and disappeared on the other side into the field.

Joe now had full command of his pack of hounds who were all around him. He praised them collectively and individually. Some of the hounds jumped up, licking his hands. When the field led by Bruce trotted up to where the pack was, the hounds were all milling around Joe and looking adoringly up at him. Limping slightly, Joe then walked his hounds slowly across the road and into the field. He went on down to the earth of the

Apricot Fox. The field followed a little way behind. When the hounds got to the hole, they stood about it, now baying again, some with their heads thrown back, barking enthusiastically and others trying to wiggle down into the small hole. Joe stood over the hole, one leg on either side, and blew "Gone to Earth" repeatedly down the hole, saluting the Apricot Fox, now safe after leading us over more than ten miles of the best of the Unionville country. He then called his hounds by name and praised them. Remounting, Joe leaned far out of his saddle to pat those of his hounds who jumped up or stood on their hind legs, their sterns wagging.

It had been a staggeringly good and exciting run with enough views of the Apricot Fox, enough fences, enough wide open galloping to satisfy all of my pent up winter needs and desires as well as those of the other foxhunters. Above all, the Apricot Fox was alive and well, now safe in his den. A dozen people complimented Annie Jones for having spotted the Apricot Fox. Everyone was talking about the run, the fences and, above all, Joe's almost miraculous rescue of the Apricot Fox when he looked like a goner.

Mrs. Hannum arrived and said, "Joe, well done. I am proud of what you and the Cheshire Hounds have done today. That you were able to stop the pack in full cry is a tribute to you and to them."

Joe just flashed his broadest Irish smile.

Nancy Miller came up, looking pleased. She said, "Your new horse, Liberty, has done brilliantly and you have come through intact though your enthusiasm continues to exceed your riding skill. Annie, why don't you explain to your father something about how to jump a horse properly. He has never listened to any of us."

Annie grinned and replied, "Old dog, new tricks, but I just may have a try at it."

Mrs. Hannum, seeing me, called out, "Well, Bill, and what does your Annie think of foxhunting now?"

Annie had taught Charlie to rear and paw the air a little like the Lone Ranger's horse, Silver. Annie now had Charlie rear and shouted "Hee Haw! Foxhunting is cool, Mrs. Hannum. Thank you for such a wonderful day."

She then turned to me and said, "Dad, if foxhunting is always this good and this exciting, why haven't you told me?"

I was tempted to say to Annie, "But, I have tried for years." However, I held my tongue, saying only to Annie, "I'm pleased that you have discovered the pleasures and excitement of foxhunting. As you see, the sport is in chasing, not in killing, the fox."

Annie turned to me and said simply, "Thanks, Dad, for everything over the years." That made everything worthwhile.

Everyone was still discussing the day's sport as we said "Good Night" to one another, the traditional salutation at the end of the day's hunting. Riding back to the vans, I said some silent prayers. My first was now that Annie had finally discovered foxhunting that she would be able to pursue the sport all the days of her life just as I have done for so many years and with such pleasure and with so many benefits. Second, I hoped that, with Caroline's continued support and encouragement, I myself would be able to enjoy years more of foxhunting, and, third, that Nancy Miller would be there to continue to look out for my hunting welfare, pleasure and safety. Most of all, I hoped that Mrs.

Hannum and her wonderful staff would continue to provide such fine sport for me, the foxes, the hounds and for the other foxhunters, now including Annie.

Now, that's how the winter of my discontent was dispelled, how Annie came at long last to foxhunting, and how the Apricot Fox survived to run many another day.

I drove on home. As always, Caroline was somewhat anxiously waiting for me. She could tell by my smiles that hunting had gone well and she could see that I was in one piece. She sat me right down. I recounted all the wonderful things that had happened, including, of course, the miraculous escape of the Apricot Fox due to Joe Cassidy's ability to control the Cheshire Hounds even in full cry. I told her how much Annie had enjoyed foxhunting. Caroline exclaimed, "This certainly has been a red letter day for you all the way around!"

Caroline then said, "You know, I have heard about foxhunting all my life from lots of people, but I still do not really understand it. On that winter afternoon a year ago, when you tried to explain foxhunting to my sister, Diana, and her husband, John, you said you would write a book explaining foxhunting to laymen. You have also often said you owe a heavy debt to foxhunting. Why don't you sit down right now and write a book explaining the basics of foxhunting to interested laymen such as myself so that we can learn what the sport is really about? You must include just why foxhunting is so exciting and why it is you and your friends take the awful risk that you do in chasing foxes. If you can do that, you will have performed a real service to the sport of foxhunting as well as those of us who are not able to gallop and jump as you do, and now Annie does, in pursuit of the wily red fox."

I replied, "My, dear, I will, I will, I really will."

And now I have!

CONCLUSION
THE CELESTIAL FOXCHASE

THE CELESTIAL FOXCHASE

God forbid that I should go to any heaven in which there were no horses.
ROBERT BONTINE CUNNINGHAM-GRAHAM

If you, the patient reader, are still with me, you have learned something about foxhunting, more accurately called foxchasing. But please do not think you have done anything with this book but skim the surface. You have only had a little taste or a sniff. Neither hearing about foxhunting nor even reading about it can nearly approximate actually doing it. In addition, a prescient reader, such as yourself, surely now knows that foxhunting is an art: that is, the pitting of the skill of the Huntsman and his hounds against the wiliness of the fox. The Huntsman must carefully assess the entire situation, the country, the scent, the wind, the temperature, the known or rumored whereabouts of foxes, and then carefully cast his hounds, but only after ensuring that the fox has fair warning from the blast on the horn and a fair lead. Then a balanced contest ensues—the chase itself: the whole object of the sport. It culminates, not in the death of the fox but in the disappearance of the fox when the fox decides he has had enough and goes to the safety and shelter of an earth.

This book started with "My Recurrent Dream." Now, it's time to find out how the dream came out. I left off as my horse was about to jump a big fence where we both had fallen the last time we tried to jump it.

. . . My horse clears the big fence. Once safely down on the other side, we gallop together with the rest of the field all the way up to the top of the big hill. Ahead of me I hear the Huntsman's horn encouraging the hounds in full cry. When we get to the top of the hill, the hounds in the distance check for a moment. I pause there while the rest of the

William Prickett on Babar. Photographer: James Graham, Montchanin, Delaware.

field gallops on. The sun is about to go down in the west behind the hills and valleys that I had hunted through for years with so much pleasure. As I stand there, my horse's flanks heaving from the brisk gallop up the hill, I pause to savor the moment.

Then the hounds open once again. The fox has turned and is heading back my way. In fact, I see the hounds coming back towards the old quarry where, long ago, stone had been dug out to build Wyeth-type houses. As I sit there watching, the fox runs out this way and that. Then he heads directly towards the quarry. The blue Jeep is there, well to one side, its doors open. The Jack Russell is frisking about. The small woman stands there halloing and pointing to where the fox is going.

The hounds come on in full cry, so close a blanket can be spread over them. Not far behind them is the Huntsman leaning forward in his stirrups, one hand holding his reins, the other hand pressing his bright copper horn to his lips. He repeatedly blows the strident notes of "Gone Away." Behind the Huntsman, and to either side and heading towards the quarry face, are the two hard riding whips followed by the Field Master, pressed hard by the field.

When the fox reaches the edge of the quarry, he puts in a bound and leaps high into the air. I expect to see him go tumbling down to the bottom of the quarry. But he finds his aerial footing and continues to scamper gradually upward and away from the pursuing hounds. When the hounds reach the edge of the quarry, instead of stopping, they too jump from the edge of the quarry right up into the air and continue upward. Surely the Huntsman will leave off blowing his horn, check his racing horse and slide to a stop. But no, not at all: when he gets to the edge of the steep rocky cliff, his horse continues galloping swiftly upward followed by the two whips, the Field Master and the field. As I sit there looking up, the fox leads the hounds, baying all the while, swiftly upward in great sweeping circles. The field, tightly bunched, keeps on pressing the Field Master who is not fifty feet behind the Huntsman. Far to one side, the blue Jeep bumps and lurches through the winter sky.

In gently ascending circles, the whole hunt continues upward and finally disappears in the wintery white clouds. The music of the hounds grows dimmer and dimmer. Then only the faintest staccato calls from the horn can be heard. At last, there is almost total silence: all that can be heard is the sound of the winter wind whistling through the tall grass all around my horse's feet. All that can be seen is the pale winter sun sinking in the west.

William Prickett on Babar. Photographer: James Graham, Montchanin, Delaware.

ACKNOWLEDGMENTS

I express my appreciation to Dorry Ross of the University of Delaware who did a superlative job in editing this volume.

As always, I express my thanks to my secretary, Phyllis Zehr, who has patiently typed and retyped drafts of *Risk in the Afternoon* under trying circumstances.

I express my appreciation to those who read and commented on the manuscript, Peter Winants, HFM; Betsy James Wyeth; Truman Welling; Mrs. John B. Hannum, MFH; and C. Martin Woods, III, MFH and his wife, Daphne, all of whom saved me from my many errors.

As always, my wife, Caroline, was instrumental in getting the book actually done and published.

William Prickett